Coffee *with* God

Coffee *with* God

ENJOY TIME OUT EACH DAY IN THE PSALMS

CWR

Compiled by Liesel Parkinson on behalf of The Armed Forces' Christian Union

'This book is the ideal tool for the Christian woman, connected in some way to the Military: to be reminded of the fact that she is not alone in her experience; that there are those who face similar difficulties alongside her; that her life is understood, if only by those who have borne the same load; and above all, that she has a God who has promised to stand by her, protect her and love her through it all.'

General Srilal Weerasooriya, President of the Association of Military Christian Fellowships

'God knows exactly what each of us needs on any particular day: comfort, challenge, courage, a different perspective, reassurance, warning, new hope. Those who use this resource will be amazed at how relevant the day's reading can be for them. Its power comes from two sources. First, the Bible itself – when we ask God to speak to us through His Word and listen expectantly, He uses even a few verses to equip us for that day. Secondly, the first hand experience of others in similar situations who have heard God speaking to them will help to direct the reader's thoughts and prayers. The few minutes of reflection each day through using *Coffee with God* will be invaluable to all those who use it, and for some it will be life changing.'

Nicky and Sila Lee, co-authors of *The Marriage Book* and *The Parenting Book*

'This is a beautifully written collection of stories based around the Psalms. They speak of passion, loss, pride and even humour. Ultimately, they all speak of the depth of God's love. I commend them to the wider Armed Forces' community. I trust they will encourage many in their own journey of faith, particularly in facing the challenges of Service life.'

The Reverend Scott J Brown QHC, Chaplain of the Fleet

'I am delighted to endorse *Coffee with God*. I recognise the outstanding contribution women make to the Services' community ... and these reflections are windows into the light and love of God. There is a deep need to take time every day to be with God, to study the Word of God and pray ... This little book of reflections draws on the great Scriptural tradition and the reflections represent a wellspring of love and prayer. I have no doubt that all who take time to use this book to support their lives will be greatly refreshed and nurtured in their Christian faith.'

The Reverend Jonathan Woodhouse QHC, Chaplain General, HM Land Forces

'Separation is a way of life for military families, and while there are many resources for those on operational duty I am delighted that we now have something written for those who remain at home as well as on the front. This book, written from experience, reveals how faith has sustained the writers in both contexts. I commend it wholeheartedly, praying that as you read it with your coffee, you may discover that same faith in our Lord Jesus Christ who brings new life and sustains us on our spiritual journey.'

The Venerable Ray Pentland QHC, RAF Chaplain-in-Chief

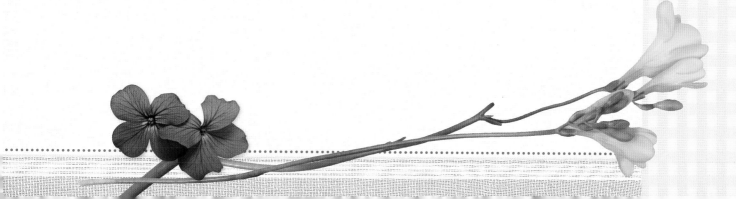

Copyright © Armed Forces' Christian Union, 2012

Published 2012 by CWR, Waverley Abbey House, Waverley Lane, Farnham, Surrey GU9 8EP, UK. Registered Charity No. 294387. Registered Limited Company No. 1990308.

The rights of all contributors to their own writings have been asserted by them in accordance with the Copyright, Designs and Patents Act 1988.

For a list of our National Distributors visit www.cwr.org.uk

Unless otherwise indicated, all Scripture references are from the Holy Bible: New International Version (NIV), copyright © 1973, 1978, 1984 by the International Bible Society.

Other Scripture quotations are marked:

GNB: *Good News Bible*, copyright © American Bible Society 1966, 1971, 1976, 1992, 1994.

NASB: *New American Standard Bible*. Scripture taken from the NEW AMERICAN STANDARD BIBLE®, Copyright © 1960, 1962, 1963, 1968, 1971, 1972, 1973, 1975, 1977, 1995 by the Lockman Foundation. Used by permission.

NKJV: *New King James Version*, © 1982, Thomas Nelson Inc.

NLT: Scripture quotations marked NLT are taken from the *Holy Bible*, New Living Translation, copyright © 1996, 2004. Used by permission of Tyndale House Publishers, Inc., Wheaton, Illinois 60189. All rights reserved.

The Message: Scripture taken from *The Message*. Copyright © 1993, 1994, 1995, 1996, 2000, 2001, 2002. Used by permission of NavPress Publishing Group.

TLB: *The Living Bible*, © 1971, 1994, Tyndale House Publishers

Concept development by Liesel Parkinson on behalf of Armed Forces' Christian Union

Editing, design and production by CWR

Printed in China by 1010 Printing

ISBN: 978-1-85345-841-5

Contents:

Acknowledgements

This collection of daily reflections would not have been possible without the dedication and commitment of the wonderful ladies who agreed to write frankly about their own experiences of military life and the role their Christian faith has played in it. I would like to thank them in particular for their perseverance and patience and their desire to give freely of themselves; turn to the back pages to meet the authors. I also really appreciate the hours of collective prayer that went into the project by members of the Armed Forces' Christian Union (AFCU). There were many times when I felt that support in a tangible way. I also need to say thank you to the lovely people who gave up their time to proofread, edit and re-write parts of the manuscript; they include, Dee Balshaw, Val Hall, Julie Knox, Hayley Palmer, Vicky Roberts, Natalie Sawtell, Kate Smith, and my own husband, Rhett, my biggest fan and sternest critic! However, the biggest thanks need to go to Caroline Maggs; without her tireless input, unflagging loyalty and creative genius, this project would never have been possible.

Liesel Parkinson

Foreword

In an interview with *The New Yorker* magazine in 1929, decorated World War One hero, journalist and Nobel Prize winning author, Ernest Hemingway was asked: 'Exactly what do you mean by guts?' He answered, 'I mean, grace under pressure.'

Courage is grace under pressure. In *Coffee with God*, writing from their personal experiences of Service life, Liesel Parkinson and twenty-seven friends show us what grace under pressure looks like – and how, as Christians operating in different spheres, each may cultivate this.

The contributors know exactly what it means to be put under pressure. They are all courageous women connected with the Military in some way, and they have learned the hard way, through hard times, in hard places, what the Bible means when it says

'... David strengthened himself in the LORD ...' (1 Sam. 30:6, NASB).

In 165 memorable meditations on the Psalms, enough for six a week for a duration of six months (the Military think in terms of six-month deployments), we are given a vision of God's faithfulness and shown how to follow Him faithfully.

However, though written by 'military' women, this is certainly not a book *only* for women or those associated with the Armed Forces. Every Christian, whatever their age or stage will find themselves nourished by these daily studies, and whatever pressures they may be faced with, in *Coffee with God*, they will undoubtedly be graced.

Simon Ponsonby,
Pastor of Theology, St Aldate's Church, 2012

Introduction

Six months can seem like a very long time, especially when separated from loved ones. Imagine then, the luxury of a daily chat with a special friend over a good cup of coffee, thinking about life, God, and how on earth they relate to the Military!

This little book of daily reflections has been specially written for you: women with a military connection. You might be a wife, girlfriend, sister or mother, patiently waiting for a sailor, marine, soldier or airman to come home. Equally, you might be a servicewoman deployed on operations, leaving friends and family behind.

Although each of the twenty-eight women in this book writes anonymously from their own experience of Service life, you can find out more about them by reading their individual biographies in the closing pages. Their stories reflect the ups and downs of their personal journeys, as they try to live out their faith in the Armed Forces, with all its excitement, frustrations, camaraderie and loneliness.

Our prayer is that this book will help you to meet with God through His Word, and that you will experience His amazing love and support as you allow Him to accompany you on your journey.

Liesel Parkinson and friends

Getting the most out of this book

There are many ways in which you can use this book, but, in order to get the most out of it, we suggest you read it with a coffee in one hand and a Bible in the other. The reflections in this book focus around the Book of Psalms. In addition a complementary passage is also given daily to act like a telescope and bring focus and clarity to the real-life stories. We suggest you read the Bible passages first.

If you read six reflections a week, this book will last you six months. In that time you will have covered the entire Book of Psalms. You will see that there are six reflections for every week marked on your 'chuff chart' (included in this book), which you can use to count down the days or keep track of those you have completed! There is also a glossary at the end to translate some of the military jargon into 'civvie-speak' – should you need it.

The reflections in the book are real-life stories which show how a bunch of ordinary women have drawn strength, freedom, healing and encouragement from God's Word. As you read about the joys, sorrows, hopes and fears expressed in these stories and by the psalmists all those years ago, we hope that you will also be able to share your own feelings, however raw, with God each day.

That is why each page concludes with a prayer or point to ponder; these are not intended to be complete prayers in themselves, but a suggestion to help lead you into your own prayers. You could complete all the reading material each day in under ten minutes, but we recommend that you treat the time in the same way you would if you were having a chat with a friend, and enjoy pausing for a moment to reflect on what God is doing in *your* life.

DAY 1

Rooted in Him

'He is like a tree planted by streams of water, which yields its fruit in season and whose leaf does not wither. Whatever he does prospers.' (Psa. 1:3)

As a young Lieutenant, I spent the toughest six months of my life at sea operationally deployed in the Gulf. It was only my second frontline posting. I shared a cabin with the only other girl on board, and in an unrelenting environment there were many pressures to test me. It was undoubtedly my faith that got me through, like the roots of the tree in this psalm. I can see how God sustained me. One day we stopped in Bahrain. It was Easter, and I went ashore to find a church. The sight that greeted me was totally unexpected – literally thousands of Christians, so many the police had to stop the traffic, flocking from every corner of the city to celebrate the Easter service! I was overwhelmed by the welcome I received. Even though I didn't know anyone, they ushered me right to the front row. God knew how much I needed that 'nugget' of encouragement.

I am reminded in this psalm, that if I obey God and resist the influence of people, activities or things that discredit Him, I will be blessed and He will watch over me. The simple message here is that the more time we spend with God, the more fruitful we become. I drew strength from God's living Word during that tough six months at sea. Whilst the storm raged among the branches, I remained 'rooted in Him' and it was His strength that carried me through. Even when we feel weak, or our faith feels so fragile, He will sustain us.

Lord Jesus, help me to spend time reading Your Word, so that my roots will grow deep. Amen.

DAY 2

Do you look at the news some days and despair? I sometimes think, 'What is the world coming to?' This psalm echoes those thoughts as it describes people who have lost respect for God and therefore for each other. But in the middle, verse 6 brings hope, 'I have installed my King …' The psalm continues to describe how all will eventually know the reign of this King, Jesus. Jesus has authority over the whole world and it is He to whom I bring my despair.

As a mum I teach my children delayed gratification (parenting buzzwords!). 'If you finish your tea, you'll get a story after bath-time.' As an Army wife I get frustrated by other despairing thoughts; 'Will we ever get our own house, or shall I have my own career?' I have realised that I too must practise delayed gratification. And not just in those things. The reading

A bigger picture

'Ask of me, and I will make the nations your inheritance, the ends of the earth your possession.' (Psa. 2:8)

from Revelation boasts of the glorious hope that will one day be fulfilled when God will live on earth with His people. That is a delayed gratification that will be *worth* the trials, the suffering and all the waiting in this life. We can look forward expectantly to the day when God will wipe away every tear and gather every son and daughter who overcomes. This prompts me to remember that despite the ever changing addresses or the different jobs or the despair that I sometimes feel, King Jesus is constant *and* in charge.

Dear Jesus, thank You that You are close to me. Thank You that You bring me peace in the midst of my daily frustrations. Amen.

DAY 3

PSALM 3;
ROMANS 12:17–19

Whilst deployed on operations in Bosnia I was part of a small team travelling around the country doing a survey to establish trigonometric stations (trig points), for use by the Allies and then later by the Bosnians. Most of the people we met were friendly and we had some interesting conversations with lots of gesticulations!

One day a member of the Mujahideen approached my colleague and me and engaged us in conversation. Before long I realised he was bragging about having killed a number of people with his knife, which he then held against my throat. For a while I was pretty terrified and at a loss as to what to do. I even considered trying to shoot him but decided he'd be able to kill me first. Then I remembered that a friend had given me some children's Winnie the Pooh cutlery, which was in my pocket. I was able to show him the very

Peace to all

'From the LORD comes deliverance. May your blessing be on your people.' (Psa. 3:8)

rounded knife and, in very basic language, joke that his knife was much sharper than mine! The situation was diffused and he ambled away, much to my relief.

Whether it is a potential threat to life or an angry exchange with a neighbour or colleague, as Christians we are called to live life differently – not to fear and escalate tensions or violence, but to find ways to bring God's blessing and His peace.

Lord, thank You that You set us the example to love our enemies and to bring peace to all. I'm sorry for the times when I've put my own emotions before Your commands. Help me to put this into practice in my daily life. Amen.

DAY 4

A good night's sleep!

'I will lie down and sleep in peace, for you alone, O Lord, make me dwell in safety.'
(Psa. 4:8)

My husband was away on an overnight trip to another RAF base and I was alone in the house. I was awoken during the night by my bed shaking. I later discovered a number of my neighbours had jumped out of bed in a panic and rushed downstairs, turning on all the lights. Meanwhile I remember thinking 'Oh an earthquake,' turning over, wondering whether I should be worried, deciding not to be and promptly falling back to sleep. As I was in Lincolnshire and not an earthquake zone, such events were pretty rare! On hearing other people's accounts of that night and their panic and confusion, I realised that God had indeed granted me a peaceful and safe night's sleep.

It's not always easy to sleep and get rest when we are alone at night, especially if we have children in the house for whom we are solely responsible. Our problems often seem so much more overwhelming during the night than in the warm light of day. We can feel alone and vulnerable. And yet the psalmist reminds us of the Lord's ability to protect us and keep us safe. We can be assured that the Lord never sleeps or slumbers but is always watching over us. Before you put your head on the pillow, or during the quiet hours of the night, ask the Lord to come and give you His peace and to bring sleep.

'Save us O Lord, while waking, and guard us while sleeping, that awake we may watch with Christ and asleep may rest in peace.'* Amen.

---

*David Stancliffe, *Celebrating Daily Prayers*, (London: Continuum, 2005) p.241.

DAY 5

I love being at the top of a high hill or a mountain, that sense of being above it all – not that I get the chance to do much walking nowadays, what with children and housework and life in general. But it's good when I can. However, I have often been caught out when the cloud has come down and covered the hill, or heavy rain has appeared from nowhere. At times like this, it's good to find shelter in the rocks – a place of refuge. On a visit once to Stirling, I looked up at the castle which has been built on the surrounding rock. It amazed me how it had been built without any of our modern technology and techniques. But times were dangerous then and a well-built, naturally-fortified castle was worth more than gold.

We often face storms in our lives: times when we need somewhere to hide or shelter; times perhaps when we are left

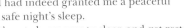

A place of refuge

'But let all who take refuge in you be glad; let them ever sing for joy. Spread your protection over them, that those who love your name may rejoice in you.' (Psa. 5:11)

to face life on our own and have to carry the family with us as our 'other halves' are away on exercise or tour. In the words of the great hymn by Richard Bewes, so stirringly used in the film *The Dam Busters*, 'God is our strength and refuge, our present help in trouble'.* If we ask Him, God will be our refuge from the storms of life. He promises to be with us always and just like the fortified castle, it is a place more precious than gold.

Lord, please be my refuge and shelter me from everything going on around me; all the things I can't control, that make life so difficult. Give me peace and strength to face the day. Amen.

*Words © Richard Bewes / Administered by The Jubilate Group, Kitley House, St Katherines Road, Torquay, Devon TQ1 4DE copyrightmanager@jubilate.co.uk USED BY PERMISSION.

DAY 6

PSALM 6;
HEBREWS 12

When I was on operations in Kabul, I had the privilege of visiting a boys' orphanage. Life for many orphaned children in Afghanistan is tough. I was horrified by the conditions in which these children had to live – no heating, no clothes, no toys, no loving parent, mould and damp and lice infestations ... Where was their rescue? Who had shown them mercy? This was deprivation at its very worst and as I reflected on the plight of these children I found myself thinking of the times when we have to experience suffering which challenges our faith and makes us question God's sovereignty in our lives. Perhaps we have been wronged by someone; this can be such a difficult place to be and can affect our health and wellbeing as we struggle with a sense of injustice.

However, unlike those young boys, we *do* have a loving parent to rescue us. God

Be merciful to me

'Turn, O LORD, and deliver me; save me because of your unfailing love.' (Psa.6:4)

might let us endure hardship, but we do know that He is a loving Father who cares about everything in our lives. Hebrews 12:6 says '... the Lord disciplines those he loves, and he punishes everyone he accepts as a son'. How wonderful to know that He sees us as His children! Suffering is an inevitable part of life but we can take heart as we remember Jesus endured the harshest discipline for us at the cross. Scripture also tells us that if we fix our eyes on Jesus anything we endure will produce a 'harvest of righteousness and peace for those who have been trained by it' (Heb. 12:11).

Lord, strengthen my feeble arms and weak knees. Make my path level so that I can be healed. Amen.

DAY 7

PSALM 7;
HEBREWS 2:1

Hearts and minds

'O righteous God, who searches minds and hearts ...' (Psa. 7:9)

As a junior female officer, I love living in the Mess – it is great fun to have the company of lots of 'fit young men in uniform'! However, there have been times when the Mess can be a difficult place as my very feminine desire to support and listen has been misleading and I have given out the wrong signals. The risk of falling into sexual sin has become all too real or as the psalmist puts it in verse 15, 'He who digs a hole and scoops it out, falls into the pit he has made'.

During times when we, or those around us, are vulnerable, we must be vigilant to guard our thoughts. God searches our minds and can reveal sinful desires. We need to test these against His Word, so that we do not stray from the truth (Heb. 2:1). I have found having another woman to be my 'accountability partner' with whom I can

be brutally honest, is a real help. Her job is to ask me very honest questions, and provide an objective external analysis of the situation; to hold up a mirror that prompts me to ask myself difficult questions, and helps me hear God. Journalling also helps me listen to what God might be saying. While it is true that God will not tempt us beyond what we can bear, and always provides a way out (1 Cor. 10:13), it is up to us to find that escape route and then to use it!

Father God, please help me to be honest with myself about my thoughts, feelings and motives. Test them, and prove them, so that I do not stray from Your truth. Amen.

DAY 8

PSALM 8;
EPHESIANS 2:6–10

No doubt you have been amazed by the beauty and power of nature, be it a magnificent sunset, the delicate complexity of a snowflake or a powerful thunderstorm. When I consider the vastness, and sheer brilliance of our universe, like David in this psalm I am filled with awe at God's majesty, glory and power. But simultaneously I am sometimes overwhelmed by my own smallness and apparent insignificance. In fact, I have at times experienced feelings of worthlessness.

As a teenager I often walked with friends to the top of a hill near my home. I remember looking down on the moonlit city below, with all its sparkling lights, and up at the beautiful night sky with its array of stars twinkling above me. But, rather than be filled with praise for God's greatness, I would wrestle with questions

Significant to Him

'When I consider your heavens, the work of your fingers, the moon and the stars, which you have set in place, what is man that you are mindful of him?' (Psa. 8:3–4)

such as, 'Why should God bother about me?' As an Army wife these feelings return, particularly when moving to an entirely new and unfamiliar environment when it's easy to feel isolated and 'lost'. This psalm and the reading from Ephesians have helped me to understand how God considers me. God has crowned each of us with glory and honour. *Wow!* We are all His workmanship, made in His image. When I remember that He knows me intimately and cares for me deeply, I am reassured that, to Him, I am very significant! I, too, want to shout, 'How majestic is His name in all the earth!'

Almighty God, who reigns over all the earth, thank You for loving me. Reign in me, be Lord of all that I am, that I might reflect Your amazing love to others. Amen.

DAY 9

PSALM 9;
DEUTERONOMY 31:6

There have been times when my work in the Military has been scary. Often those fears have not been to do with enemy action, but stem from my own fears about trusting other people. Fears of being left behind, or abandoned by the very men who are supposed to be protecting me, are very real (although of course I don't mention this to them!). This can be similar to the fears we may have when our husbands disappear off on duty. For some people, the ongoing threat of abandonment may invoke anxiety that they experienced as a child, perhaps times when they felt forgotten or let down.

God challenges us to take refuge in Him; to let go of the reins; to trust Him totally. I am encouraged to do this when I read that He has *never* let down those who are seeking Him. I notice that it doesn't say 'He has never forsaken those who are

Never forsaken

'... for you, LORD, have never forsaken those who seek you.' (Psa. 9:10)

good at praying and reading their Bible, and never feel anxious, or get scared', it simply says that He will never forsake those who *seek* Him. We also hear this promise way back in Deuteronomy.

To never forsake means to never abandon, never desert, never leave, never give up on, never disown, never discard, never dump, never leave stranded, never cast aside. Rather, God promises to return to and stay with those who seek Him. When I am fearful and choose to speak these words aloud, there can be an incredible sense of security and of being in God's presence. Try it for yourself today.

Father God, when I fear abandonment, may I sense Your unending presence wrapped around me. Amen.

DAY 10

In the waiting time

'God, are you avoiding me? Where are you when I need you?' (Psa. 10:1, *The Message*)

I find that problems often occur when my husband goes away on deployment or exercise. It's only then that the car begins to sing, the electrics come alive, the washing machine leaks or the computer needs rebooting. I can't just phone him up and say 'Help! – blue job!' I often lose sight of the fact that God is with me and is trying to show me that He cares about these problems that I am facing. All too regularly I find that it is me choosing only to see the worst of the situation. I ignore His whisper in my heart, 'Hold on My child, wait, be of good courage.' It's the very last thing I want to hear so I brush it away and continue to rage.

However, at those times when I do choose to stop what I am doing and seek God for a while, I see that there have been many little ways in which He has been showing me that He is *always constant*; the parking space just outside the shops, green traffic lights all the way home, or a friend who phones up for a cheerful chat. These are inextricably linked with His continued care because He knows these things are important to me. I am learning that the problems will come but when I take the time to 'wait' on God, I find He has *not* left me but has in fact been blessing me in many small things that give my life value and meaning.

Dear Father, please help me to remember and appreciate that You are a loving 'constant' in my life despite how I may feel about it. Amen.

DAY 11

Last year I was sent a calendar with Bible verses on it. I thought it would be a good way for the family to learn Scripture so I hung it in the downstairs toilet. It was working beautifully until August when the text read; 'Nothing in all creation is hidden from God's sight' (Heb. 4:13). My children became bashful overnight!

Psalm 11 has a similar line, 'He observes everyone on earth; his eyes examine them' (v.4). I don't know about you, but when I first read this, it made me feel very uneasy. A bit like being on *Big Brother* – which means you can never relax and enjoy a moment of quiet, even if it comes your way! But God isn't 'Big Brother'. He isn't watching and waiting for you to mess up so He can mock you with it and punish you. In 1 John 4 we read about true love. It's worth reading the whole chapter but I would like to highlight verse 18:

The look of love

'The LORD is in his holy temple;
the LORD is on his heavenly throne.
He observes everyone on earth; his eyes
examine them.' (Psa. 11:4, NIV, 2011)

• •

'There is no fear in love, but perfect
love casts out fear, because fear involves
punishment' (NASB). So take heart in the
thought that God is watching you, He is
watching you with love in His heart. He
isn't willing you to fail, He is watching
so He can help you when you do. He is
watching and waiting for you to call out for
help; then He will be with you and will fill
you with His love.

----

*Lord thank You that You are watching over
me. Help me to call on You for everything
I need. Take away my fear of what lies
ahead and fill me with Your love. Amen.*

DAY 12

PSALM 12;
2 CORINTHIANS 9:8

• •

I am currently posted with an overseas Air
Force. It has been a difficult experience –
one that took me completely by surprise.
It is a spiritually dry environment and
living alone in a foreign country has been
very isolating. I work alongside a self-
confirmed atheist who likes to debate why
it is impossible for God to exist. Making
friends has never been a major issue,
but here I have faced rejection – from
uncomplimentary notes left on my desk to
being openly excluded from events. It has
been a lonely and painful time in which
I have questioned God's will for me in all
this. But, I also realise that God has put a
responsibility on my shoulders. God loves
His people and it breaks His heart that so
many are lost. I am His representative here.

In the Gospels, Jesus said '… take up
[your] cross and follow me' (Matt. 16:24).
That is no guarantee of an easy ride! In

Being faithful

'Help, LORD, for the godly are no more;
the faithful have vanished from
among men.' (Psa.12:1)

• •

trying to follow Jesus instead of the world,
I will always face reactions from people
who don't see why I try to live this way.
But, in trying not to respond in anger to
what has happened and in acknowledging
where I have gone wrong, I am perhaps
giving people their only opportunity to
see the loving nature of our heavenly
Father. When it gets difficult, I remember
the Jews during the Exodus. Desert life
was hard and they often doubted God's
purpose, but He always provided and was
always faithful. In my desert experience,
when I also doubt the Lord, I remember
that *He always rescues His people.*

----

*Father, help me to be one of Your faithful
among men. Amen.*

DAY 13

PSALM 13;
LUKE 15:23–24

The short way back

'But I trust in your unfailing love; my heart rejoices in your salvation.' (Psa. 13:5)

DAY 14

PSALM 14;
GALATIANS 5:19–24

When I was a child, we once visited some relatives in Yorkshire. After lunch, we walked along a river path for two hours until we reached our cousins' house, where we had tea. At 8pm my parents announced that it was time to go back to the farmhouse for bed. It was dark outside and I was horrified at the thought of having to walk all that way home. As I voiced my concern my family burst out laughing, and to my relief, told me that the two houses were only 50 metres apart. Our afternoon walk had been a long meander rather than the straight path between the two houses. The return trip took just five minutes!

In my military career I've often felt like I've wandered a long way from God and that it would take me ages to find my way back. This is especially so when I've been isolated from fellowship or been too busy with everything else. But the truth is however far we feel from God, we don't have to retrace our long journey to get back to Him, we just have to take a few steps. If we trust in Him and repent of our sins, in His mercy He will forgive us, and through grace restore us. In Luke 15 the parable of the Prodigal Son shows how the father watches longingly for the son to return and as soon as he sees him, he rushes to meet him and forgives him.

Thank You God for Your endless love: I'm sorry for the things that have caused separation from You and I ask for Your forgiveness today, my loving Father and faithful Friend. Amen.

Those serving in the Military are likely to see suffering in a way that others will never experience. Perhaps that is why so many I have met have come to the conclusion that there is no God. But much of the suffering in this world doesn't come from the fact that God doesn't exist, rather that we choose to deny His existence and act contrary to His divine nature. When we do this we become the opposite of what God created us for. The result is war, sickness, grief, pain and personal conflict. What God wants is a loving, committed relationship with us, and for us to have that with each other.

Don't be foolish. Denial of God ultimately leads to eternal separation from Him and all that is good. To acknowledge God and follow Him brings the fruit of the Spirit in increasing measure and a sure hope of eternal life.

Acknowledge God

'The fool says in his heart, "There is no God".' (Psa. 14:1)

My own experience of life before Christ, particularly when I was in the RAF, was one of sexual immorality, hatred and selfish ambition and an increasing measure of unhappiness and worthlessness. Once I committed my life to Christ, I began to experience a greater sense of hope and worth. Life started to make sense. It was Jesus who gave me back my self-respect and showed me that I mattered. Is there anything stopping you believing in the One who died for you and has risen from the dead to bring you forgiveness and eternal life?

Lord Jesus with You there is fullness of life. Please help me to trust You and acknowledge that You exist and want to be intimately involved in my life. Amen.

DAY 15

PSALM 15;
JAMES 2:22–24

Early into our first posting overseas, we were invited to our Commanding Officer's house for an informal lunch. We were both worried as my newly promoted Lance Corporal husband had never had to have much interaction with the Colonel before. He didn't sleep the night before and was freshly pressed, clean shaven and neatly dressed next morning in preparation. Lunch was a success. Conversation flowed and we found that both families had a lot in common. So much so that it became a frequent event after that at either house.

The psalmist worries about whether he is good enough for God's guest list. Perhaps he (like some of us) sees God as being like the CO, rather than a close friend. Would I worry if I invited 'Commanding-Officer-God' for dinner? Yes! How could I make conversation with someone who already knows what I am

Jelly for pudding

'God, who gets invited to dinner at your place? How do we get on your guest list?' (Psa. 15:1, *The Message*)

thinking? I would have to use my best dinner service – the one with matching cups! I might clean so deep that the house became immaculate; difficult with small children! I would consider the menu for a long while. But if I was inviting my good friend God for dinner then I would be looking forward to it. We would eat potluck, probably with jelly for pudding, and not be worried about mismatching crockery. I would ask Him those things I have been contemplating while woolgathering. Why is it so colourful at the bottom of the ocean when no one ever goes there? Why can I not touch my elbow to my nose? And my friend God and I would laugh together.

Lord, help me to enjoy my down-time with You, my friend. Amen.

DAY 16

Squeezed hard

'I keep my eyes always on the Lord. With him at my right hand, I will not be shaken.'
(Psa. 16:8, NIV, 2011)

I first left my home in the Caribbean to fly to the UK to study. None of my family had ever done this before and if I had been given the choice then, I would not have done it. But with thoughts to my future my parents decided this was the next step. The excitement warred with the terror of the unknown inside me and indigestion won! The day I arrived at my college was wintry, the mist hung over the willows which dotted the grounds. A ghost or two at the gate would have completed the picture! I thought, 'Lord, why? I could be at home on the beach now!' I grew up in a Christian family and I knew my faith was being tested. How much did I truly believe in Scripture and the promises that had been drilled into me from Sunday School? Was God truly 'worth His salt' or was it all words to spout when life was good?

A test of faith like this can make one stronger or cause one to fall. I can see how gently God has held me and shown me His deep love in the midst of many anxious times. Like a teabag, I have found strength comes with squeezing! There are plenty of opportunities for squeezing in the Military! Both Psalm 16 and the passage from 2 Samuel encourage us to trust God and keep going when the going is tough. If I was given the choice today would I still make the same life choices? Yes, because of the knowledge that I am securely held by Him.

Lord, thank You that with You, I am complete. Amen.

DAY 17

After being related a tale of woe about missed opportunities caused by opposition from a line manager, a friend replied that we should pray that the manager prospers and has a promotion! Talk about conversation stoppers! It is easy to forget sometimes that we are in a spiritual battle and respond out of our own hurt, rather than acting as Christ would have us do. As 2 Corinthians 10:3 says: 'For though we live in the world, we do not wage war as the world does.' Instead we need to have the 'mind of Christ' (1 Cor. 2:16).

When we throw our weapons down and give in, we miss out on seeing the greatness of our God and His power at work through us. General MacArthur is purported to have said 'The enemy is in front of us, the enemy is behind us, the enemy is to the right and to the left of us.

DAY 18

Victory ahead

'Show me the wonders of your great love, you who save by your right hand those who take refuge in you from their foes.' (Psa. 17:7, NIV, 2011)

They can't get away this time!'* However, unlike a human battle, we conquer through the power of the 'blood of the Lamb and the words of our testimony,' (Rev. 12:11). The frontal assault wave is God's arms of love. It goes against every human instinct to show love and kindness to those who willingly spite us and plan against us, but God is greater. As we 'bless those who persecute us' (Rom. 12:11), we allow God free access into the situation, giving Him permission to 'work all things together for good' (Rom. 8:28) – not just for us, but for the very people who are currently opposing us.

Lord, help me to respond with Your love today – whatever I may face. Amen.

*See: http://www.goodreads.com/quotes/show/217566/

The tunnel's end

'He brought me out into a spacious place; he rescued me because he delighted in me.' (Psa. 18:19)

There was a time in my life when I felt alone in the darkness. I felt that I needed help and went forward for some prayer ministry. I had a picture of a wall. I couldn't see over it or around it – because my nose was pressed up against it. It seemed like the bricks of the wall were the issues and problems, real and imagined, that I was facing. As I was prayed for, it seemed that Jesus led me back away from the wall – and I realised that the wall was not much higher than I was tall. As I moved back and up a slight slope, I could see the sun, and trees and fields on the other side. Then I noticed that the wall had a gate in it a bit further along. Jesus took my hand and led me through the gate into the beautiful fields beyond.

God taught me that He doesn't necessarily take the problems away (or demolish the wall!) but He can help us to get things into perspective and lead and guide us, showing us the way *through* the problems. Psalm 18 is a wonderful testimony by David to God's faithfulness in bringing him out of dark places – it contains some beautiful pictures of God's steadfastness, His power, His compassion and His justice. May we never forget to praise God for bringing us out of the dark into the spacious places, or that He delights in us as His children.

Lord, help me to remember to cry to You in times of trouble; thank You that Your love is unfailing and that You meet my deepest needs. Amen.

DAY 19

PSALM 18:25–50;
2 THESSALONIANS 2:14–17

Winning through!

'You, O Lord, keep my lamp burning; my God turns my darkness into light. With your help I can advance against a troop; with my God I can scale a wall.' (Psa. 18:28–29)

Moving, moving, moving! I don't know about you but I am in my eleventh year of marriage and currently living in my sixth house. My twins went to three different pre-schools and are now in their second primary school and may go to another two before secondary school. I know that this is the normal way of life for Service families but it doesn't make it any easier each time we see our belongings being packed into boxes.

This psalm was prayed for me during a time when we had moved twice in the same year. I was finding it hard watching my children trying to adjust and found that my own lamp was hardly burning as I tried to stay positive for everyone. For my husband it seems so much easier as he walks straight into a new job, with colleagues in the workplace. This psalm encourages me to believe the impossible.

As we place our anxieties at the foot of the cross Jesus gives us strength to advance, supernatural ability to hurdle insurmountable obstacles and light in our dark places. An element of trust is involved in knowing that we are in the place of God's will, but when we are, He will provide.

Since this time I have learnt to leave my moving worries in Jesus' care. It's not always been easy but I know He won't ever put me in a situation that I cannot cope with. (Also, I find that whenever I feel alone a Christian friend makes herself known to me.) God is amazing!

Father, may Your will be done here on earth. Let me be Your servant wherever I find myself living. Amen.

DAY 20

PSALM 19;
ISAIAH 26:3–4

My sense of direction has always been challenged. I think my greatest embarrassment to date was on Exercise in BATUS, Canada. Surrounded by rocks and mountains I often thought of God as my rock. Isaiah 26:4 says, 'Trust in the Lord forever, for the Lord ... is the Rock eternal'. On a return trip from Calgary Airport it quickly became obvious that the driver did not know the way back, and as 'the officer' I was apparently in charge. We had no map, no satellite navigation system and no phone ... not a good start.

Our jet-lagged passenger quickly fell asleep at the petrol station we stopped at to fill up. Imagine his surprise, and our embarrassment, when he woke up six hours later to find we were back at the same garage! Our road trip had nearly taken us to the Rockies, in fact it was only when we saw them looming in front of

Geographically embarrassed!

'The signposts of GOD are clear and point out the right road. The life-maps of GOD are right, showing the way to joy. The directions of GOD are plain ...'
(Psa. 19:7–8, *The Message*)

DAY 21

PSALM 20;
1 PETER 5:7

A lesson in trust

'May he give you the desire of your heart and make all your plans succeed.'
(Psa. 20:4)

us that we realised we were in fact going the wrong way! I wondered whether to pray for the mountain to be thrown into the sea (Matt. 21:21), but I didn't think it would help! It is a shame I didn't think of Psalm 19 and ask God to show us the right way, believing, as the psalmist did, that He gives straightforward and easy-to-follow directions! Instead we made our weary way back, via a stay at the airport overnight, and endured everyone's ridicule on our return.

Lord, help me to seek Your direction and revelation for my life, especially when I lose my bearings and don't know which way to go. Amen.

I often struggle to believe that God's promises for me are true. Can I really trust Him to look after those I love, emotionally and physically? Having two daughters away at boarding school and a husband in Afghanistan tests this daily. They are completely beyond my own human ability to protect them from all danger and harm; I am forced to surrender this very human desire to God who is infinitely more capable.

Then there are the everyday trust issues in which I have to choose either God's way or my own. My own definitely feels safer because I have control, but God's way is often immeasurably more satisfying in the long run and allows me to grow and develop in tangible ways.

Recently, my husband and I felt that God was asking us to leave the Army to begin some kind of full-time Christian ministry.

I wondered: could I really trust God to provide for us financially? After all, I told myself, we have so many important financial obligations, not least to the children at school. It took months of battling in prayer to make the decision, and then months of agonising, wondering if his application for redundancy would be accepted. When it was, I felt shocked and was consumed again by the old fears. However, God is always faithful to His word; within a fortnight God not only provided for the children's education, He provided me with a new laptop; a gift from wonderful Christian friends. God showed me that His plans for me will succeed and that He also knows and cares about my heart's secret desires.

Lord, let me put my trust in You. Amen.

DAY 22

Blessing others

'You welcomed him with rich blessings and placed a crown of pure gold on his head.'
(Psa. 21:3)

The Military is a place that is competitive, controlled, and sometimes difficult. As a result, it can be hard to like, forgive or bless others. In spite of this I had the most exciting twenty-six years serving in the Army while the Lord was training me for the work I do now. I made a lot of mistakes and did not always do what He told me.

Recently, whilst ministering to people who, proud and unkind, clearly did not want to be with our team, I got angry! However, the Lord told me 'to bless those that curse us' as it says in 1 Corinthians 4. I was convicted! I went and showed love and was able to do so because Jesus was there. As a result there was a remarkable change in their attitude and a huge miracle of healing took place. Had the Lord not spoken to me, my sinful anger would have prevented that healing.

In the Military we may face opposition and uncertainty but we need to be able to bless even the most difficult people. Psalm 21 paints a wonderful picture of how the Lord pours out His unmerited blessings without asking for anything in return. Sometimes we feel the establishment is controlling us and we have a struggle to bless those in authority. Obedience is key. In fact, blessing others helps us as much, if not more, than it helps the person being blessed!

Lord Jesus, release me to bless those who would treat me badly. Help me to love those who are hard to love so that You may place a crown of gold on my head. Amen.

DAY 23

It is never easy talking about our faith, especially at the beginning of a new tour. It can be particularly difficult within a new social group to speak out either against something that we know to be wrong, or to express the Christian viewpoint, especially when we feel out-ranked by those around us (irrespective of whether it's us or our husbands wearing the tabs!) We can feel inferior and fear being labelled as the 'religious nut' or being excluded from the 'in' crowd. Indeed there have been many times when I have come home from an event knowing that I should have spoken up for what I believe, but my tongue has felt stuck to the roof of my mouth and I am left without words to say.

When we feel lost for words we need to trust that God will provide the right word at the right time. The more time that we

What shall I say?

'... my tongue sticks to the roof of my mouth ...' (Psa. 22:15)

spend with God and in reading His Word the more we will hear the Spirit's voice encouraging us to speak out or to keep silent. I have also noticed that the longer I take within a tour to admit that I go to church or that I have a faith, the more difficult it is to make that first comment. So take courage and trust that God will give you the right words to speak at the right time.

Lord, as I go out into the community today, give me the courage and the wisdom to know when to speak out for You and when to keep silent, that I might be a witness of Your love to all those whom I meet. Amen.

DAY 24

PSALM 22:19–31;
1 THESSALONIANS 5:11

Shout aloud!

'I will declare your name to my people; in the assembly I will praise you.' (Psa. 22:22, NIV, 2011)

Yesterday we looked at the problem of speaking about our faith in the communities within which we live. Surely then, it should be easier to talk about our faith within our churches? Not always. Many of us have a natural tendency to be terribly 'British' about our religion, believing that it is a personal matter and not for shouting about from the rooftops. Additionally, it can sometimes feel, in our way of life, that we change churches as frequently as we change our socks (perhaps that analogy doesn't work if you have sons; I only have a daughter!). It is then hard to build up trust sufficiently with the people in church to be able to share what God is, or indeed *isn't*, doing in our lives, especially in military churches when others may 'outrank' us.

But it is such an encouragement when someone actually comes and tells you with excitement of something that God is doing in their life. I love to hear the testimonies of others that God is alive and well and doing marvellous things! Equally, it is so reassuring when people are honest and say how they are feeling when things are not going so well. It takes courage to be real. If no one else is doing that, look for an opportunity to break the ice; tell them how good God is – even if it is only that you managed to get to church that morning!

Father, thank You that we have so much to praise and give You thanks for. Help me to remind others that You are worthy of our praise, that we might be an encouragement to one another. Amen.

DAY 25

His provision is amazing

**'The Lord is my shepherd,
I shall not be in want.' (Psa. 23:1)**

My husband was re-joining the Navy as a chaplain after completing his curacy. We applied for a quarter in Plymouth and then went to view our allocation. Our hearts sank. 'Extremely run down' is the best description for it, not to mention being in an area we really didn't want to live in. We 'dared' to refuse it, which immediately sent us to the bottom of the list. People from the church prayed and gave us helpful (!) advice such as 'God often waits until the eleventh hour'. We reached 23:59!

My husband and son both needed to be in Plymouth by the beginning of September to start work and school respectively. Visiting a Christian conference, New Wine, in August for the day, my husband ran into one of his college friends who asked if he knew of anyone who needed a house. A Naval Captain from his church had gone to France for a year and his house was standing empty. We later discovered that before they left, the owners had walked around the house praying for it to be used and had even made up the beds! We stayed there for over a month, until another quarter became available – and then found God had blessed us with the perfect location and a house that was above our entitlement. What an amazing answer to prayer. So often when we have a need, it is easy to think that God has closed His ears to our requests. This can be the time when our faith is tested to the limits and we learn to trust and totally rely on Him.

Lord, thank You for providing for all our needs. Teach me to rely always upon You. Amen.

DAY 26

This psalm points us to holiness; a hard walk! My greatest challenge as a single woman working in the Army for twenty-six years was ensuring I forgave the men with whom I worked! I found a bitter root of judgment built up against men due to feeling that my opinion was not valued for being a woman; there were many unkind comments made to me because I was single and without a man. Over the years I became very defensive and would lash out to men before they hurt me and say 'put your ego away'!

I was challenged about my attitude towards men and my offensive behaviour to strike before I was attacked.

One day I realised I was at fault and needed to repent of my coping strategy which was not godly, and forgive men in line with Matthew 6:14. I did this and found it had dramatic consequences;

Forgiveness – a daily walk

'He who has clean hands and a pure heart …' (Psa. 24:4)

I was truly different. I no longer felt bitter towards men and I was free! My life changed and I had clean hands and a pure heart! But it wasn't a one off; it became a daily walk for me. I had to *keep forgiving* and not allow any bitterness to take root and affect my relationship with Jesus. Men still made unkind comments but with Jesus' help, forgiveness became gradually easier.

Lord Jesus, help me daily to walk in forgiveness and allow You to be the judge of people who may hurt me. Enable me to forgive them so that I may be clean and pure. Amen.

DAY 27

PSALM 25;
EPHESIANS 2:4–5

Having a perfectionist father, I grew up with the impression that I was loved more for the things I achieved, and less when my performance (be it academic, sporting or behavioural) was deemed 'disappointing'. Being a female officer in the Royal Engineers, working in a male-dominated environment, I also felt that I had to perform better than everyone else in order to gain equal credibility. I thus struggled with the mantra that 'nothing we can do will cause God to love us more and nothing we do causes Him to love us less'. But, the fact is, He does love us because we are His. He made us and He loves us, even before we acknowledge Him as Lord (Eph. 2:4–5).

I now have a month-old baby who, like all her age, is utterly helpless. I was expecting maternity leave to be endured rather than enjoyed, with all the sleep

Because He loves me

'… according to your love remember me, for you are good, O Lord.' (Psa. 25:7)

deprivation and nothing in return, for the first few months at least. However, I have been amazed at the amount I love her, even when she is uttering blood-curdling cries and I'm at a loss what to do! How much more then does our heavenly Father love each of us, as we are told in Matthew 7:10–12. In fact, nothing can separate us from His love (Rom. 8:38–39) as He delights in us (Zeph. 3:17). So instead of striving to gain His affection, let us revel in His love and overflow with it towards others.

Lord, thank You for Your unconditional love. Help me to comprehend this more fully, so that I may show Your love to others, especially those considered unlovely or unlovable. Amen.

DAY 28

Protestations

'Vindicate me, O Lord, for I have led a blameless life; I have trusted in the Lord without wavering.' (Psa. 26:1)

Do you ever feel that because you have served the Lord with your all that He owes you? Sometimes I do. I think 'Lord, look what I have done for You, in Your name. Now You must look after my interests!' But He doesn't owe me anything. He loves me so much that He died to rescue me so that He and I can be together. All I have to do now is to trust and love Him. Love *Him* for Himself and not for what He can do or provide for me.

Did Joseph, after being thrown into prison, ever think, 'God I didn't do anything wrong, what is going on here? When is it going to end?' I imagine he did. Sometimes God allows me to get into difficult situations and I realise slowly that everything I have should be His, including my responses to and in that circumstance. My integrity and purpose must be based on His Word and He will be my vindicator.

He does not owe me an easy life just because I trust and believe in Him. What will become easier, however, is how to deal with my problems as they arise so the phrase 'In God We Trust' takes on a new depth of meaning. The peace that He gives to me because I depend on His resources allows me to sleep soundly at night, not lie awake wringing my hands in despair. It doesn't mean that I am not proactive or resourceful; it means I will allow God to direct the master strategy.

Give your worries and problems over to God; He's going to be up all night anyway!

DAY 29

After many years of witnessing in a military environment, which can be rather apathetic to the gospel message, I became depressed. I was struggling with chronic ill-health and seemed always to be defending the Christian faith in a fatigued state. Being single did not help the situation as I would often go home and beat myself up over ways I could have witnessed better, with no one around to help me gain a better perspective. This eventually took its toll and I admitted to God that I didn't trust Him to heal me, find me a husband or make me fruitful for Him. He graciously looked after me while I was struggling to cope and on a number of occasions spoke quite powerfully to me through the Bible.

One day I was reading this psalm and the verses at the end just seemed to leap off the page, 'I am still confident of

DAY 30

PSALM 28;
LUKE 12:22–31

Waiting on God

'I am still confident of this: I will see the goodness of the LORD in the land of the living.' (Psa. 27:13)

this: that I will see the goodness of the LORD in the land of the living. Wait for the LORD; be strong and take heart and wait for the LORD' (Psa. 27:13–14). Days later an Army officer I knew surrendered his life to Christ whilst I sat with him in his office. As you can imagine, this was a huge encouragement to me as I saw the fulfilment of the promise. I still hold on to those verses and wait for God because I believe I will still see more of His goodness. Will you continue to trust Him when it is hard to wait? It will be worth it.

Lord Jesus, help me to surrender to You unconditionally, wait for You patiently and trust You completely. Amen.

Today I heard that a friend of a friend had died in theatre six days prior to finishing his tour. It is terrible news and, if I am honest, the scenario I most dread. It is so hard to imagine what it must be like to come to terms with the sudden ending of a life in its prime, or how I personally might cope with it. In Luke 12:25 Jesus instructed us not to worry, 'Who of you by worrying can add a single hour to his life?' The opposite of worry is trust. This is much harder to say than do. Trust is only possible if we have something (or someone) to trust in.

Recently, we've seen the historical pillars of trust in our world collapse around us; banks folding, nations on the brink of bankruptcy, earthquakes and ash clouds have all made headline news. Even closer to home our once secure 'jobs for life' have been hit by redundancies and

A shield called trust

'The LORD is my strength and my shield; my heart trusts in him, and I am helped.' (Psa. 28:7)

cuts to pensions. Psalm 28 reminds us that we can trust *in the Lord* who sustains us, surrounds us and hears us when we call. Our trust in Him is like a shield that protects our minds from fear; fear that seeks to overwhelm us and crush us.

Lord Jesus, thank You that You never leave me alone and that You care about me so much. You know the fears I have, and the burden of anxiety and worry I carry. I choose to trust in You today. Shield me from everything that would seek to rob my peace of mind. I ask this in the name of Jesus. Amen.

DAY 31

PSALM 29;
ROMANS 12:2

Lord over all creation

**'The LORD gives strength to his people; the
LORD blesses his people with peace.'**
(Psa. 29:11)

As a Troop Commander in Germany I was asked to take a UK-based troop to Norway. I was very excited, despite not knowing anyone in the other unit. They, however, had obviously heard that I was a Christian and from the outset I received some animosity. Halfway through the deployment we had completed the survey task and moved on to the arctic survival phase. The previous week the snow shelters had collapsed, burying some soldiers briefly and causing distress and worry. My group were cutting decks of cards and saying, 'If the next card is the nine of spades, then our shelter will collapse and we'll all die!' and then drawing that card.

Not knowing the soldiers very well was an advantage. In a few weeks they would return to the UK and I would return to Germany, so I had little to lose. I reached for my Bible and began reading them psalms of encouragement showing how the Lord had power over creation, and then I said a simple prayer. That night we slept in our snow shelter and in the morning we all emerged safely. Nothing more was said, but my reputation as a Bible-basher was further reinforced! You may not be in a snow shelter but whatever you or those around you fear, God can be trusted. Lean on Him and let others know who provides your strength.

Lord, thank You that we can put our trust in You, the Lord of the heavens and earth and the King over all creation. I am sorry for the times when I have not trusted You. Help me to trust You more fully today and always. Amen.

DAY 32

PSALM 30;
1 PETER 4:12–13

In training we were warned that, on arrival at our first unit, we were likely to have a trick played on us. I arrived at the Mess to be told that I was the only living-in member and that the contents of the property had been auctioned off that day, but would not be removed for some months. I was convinced this was the trick and that in a few days other young officers would appear. Sadly it wasn't so and, worse still, each night I would discover more of the auctioned items had been taken, eventually leaving me just a 24-hour honesty bar!

The loneliness in the Mess was compounded by being the only female, and the only Christian, in the unit. Consequently I was treated as an anomaly by my colleagues and as a threat by their wives. One night I was at a low and cried out to God that I could not cope with

Trust in Him

'I will exalt you, O Lord, for you lifted me out of the depths ... You turned my wailing into dancing ...' (Psa. 30:1,11)

DAY 33

PSALM 31;
GENESIS 2:2–3

Godly time management

'My life is consumed by anguish and my years by groaning; ... Since you are my rock and my fortress, for the sake of your name lead and guide me.' (Psa. 31:10,3)

one day more of this. Miraculously the very next day was so much better. There were many more bad days and weeks subsequently, but I knew that God had heard my cry and could provide relief when absolutely required. A colleague asked why I didn't just get the message and leave the unit, and I explained that I felt that God had put me there for some reason. Wonderfully, sometime later he, and then his wife, became Christians. Looking back it was all worth it, God turned my wailing into dancing!

Lord, thank You that You never leave us even when we cannot see or feel Your presence. Thank You for bringing hope out of despair and revealing Your glory. Amen.

As I was considering themes on which to write, I was drawn to the more dramatic incidents of my military career and the ways in which God had moved through them. However, I was also reminded of the jobs I have done where the humdrum of everyday life can be just as challenging to my faith, albeit in a different way.

The constant pressure and the tight deadlines build up to produce long hours in the office. I can find at these times that the very things that will help me (physical exercise, lunch breaks and Christian fellowship) fall away and instead I succumb to the temptation to eat a sandwich at the desk, whilst doing yet more work. I fail to notice the gradual increase in workload and the detrimental effect upon both my physical and spiritual life. It is often only when family or colleagues are affected and point out

the error of my ways, that I am able to recognise the problem and then try to reverse the trend and get out of the rut I've been ploughing.

Taking some time out for prayer helps me to calm down and gives me some vital space to think, as well as allowing me the time I need to realign my priorities to God's. Amazingly, He also often intervenes to make my work more efficient so that I am able to fit both into the day!

Lord, thank You for setting us the example that You rested and enjoyed the fruits of Your creation. Sorry for the times when I have been too consumed by busyness. Help me to manage my time in accordance with Your will. Amen.

DAY 34

PSALM 32;
2 CHRONICLES 7:14

It's a choice!

'Blessed is [s]he whose transgressions are forgiven, whose sins are covered.' (Psa. 32:1)

I wonder if, like me, you are always amazed when you go into a bookshop to see how many self-help books there are, all claiming to offer quick and effective ways of gaining a happier, healthier life? For me, Psalm 32 could sit very neatly on the self-help bookshelf; however, unlike most other books, this wonderful psalm really does do what it says on the cover!

For many years I have struggled with depression as a result of carrying around sin and the guilt of that sin deep within me. The psalm so clearly reveals what keeping hold of sin does to us; it 'wastes away bones', we lack strength and we 'groan inwardly'. What a true picture of how I have felt when my depression was at its height; sapped of energy, aching and my mind full of negative thoughts. The psalm continues by revealing that we can decide to 'help ourselves' through choosing to repent and receive forgiveness for our sin. This is echoed in 2 Chronicles where God promises to hear the humble prayer of His people, to forgive their sin and to heal their land. I have found that, in practice, the pathway to freedom from depression is to nurture a lifestyle of humble repentance. Like the psalmist, I have discovered that I have been taken from the depths of despair, to a place of praise and worship where I can declare God's blessings, protection, deliverance and love.

Dear Lord Jesus, thank You that through You I am forgiven. Please help me to develop a lifestyle of repentance and to have faith to believe that I am truly forgiven. Amen.

DAY 35

PSALM 33;
PROVERBS 16:3

Planning: some of us are good at it, some of us tend to fly by the seat of our pants; some of us stick to our plans, others see them as a starting point. As many of you will have experienced, planning anything in the Military can be risky. I was tasked, along with a colleague, to allocate manpower for an exercise, and sulkily said to him, 'There's no point in making a plan, it'll only have to change a hundred times before the day.' To this he replied, 'There has to be a plan in order for there to be a change of plan.' I thought this was funny, but also true.

The reality of Service life is that we frequently have to adjust to changes in our plans a lot more readily than many other people. Today's psalm says that the Lord's plans stand solid forever, through all the generations. Often I find it difficult to see God's plan, especially when things

DAY 36

PSALM 34;
2 PETER 1:2–4

The planning phase

'But the plans of the LORD stand firm forever, the purposes of his heart through all generations.' (Psa. 33:11)

seem to change so much. But, because He formed my heart and knows my every move, I know He ultimately holds a perfect plan for a unique blueprint. Our lives do not depend on chance and luck. His plans include our future for generations to come. Proverbs 16:3 urges us to commit everything we do to God, and *He will establish our plans.* Next time you make a plan, ask God to help you to plan with His perspective and insight, so that once made it will be fulfilled, whatever the Military powers throw at it!

Father, may I hold more tightly to Your plans for my life and more loosely to the world's plans. Amen.

This verse from Psalm 34 reminds me of the love and good gifts that our heavenly Father longs to bestow on His children. Have you had prayers answered with abundance? Twelve years ago I was ready to move from my small one-bedded flat into a slightly bigger home, so I got on my knees in prayer, to ask the Lord to lead me to the flat of His choice. The Lord answered and provided the perfect home which I still love, and friends kindly say they love coming to visit. It is a haven of peace and rather too full of bears, books, cross stitch and card-making materials, amongst other things!

As an Army child I really understand the constant upheaval of moving. It's hard to turn an empty shell of a house into a real home. But our heavenly Father goes before us and prepares the way. When I moved here I asked a church elder to

Our abundant God

'Taste and see that the LORD is good, blessed is the man who takes refuge in him.' (Psa. 34:8)

come and pray in my home, in each room, to cleanse the flat from anything that might have gone before. The homes we live in have had many occupants before us and it is important to have a spiritual march-in as well as a physical one. As the Lord takes you to a new area, ask Him to bless you with new friendships and for special opportunities to blossom where you are planted.

Father God, thank You for the lavish way You answer our prayers – in ways we don't think of or expect. Give us Your grace in times of upheaval. Amen.

DAY 37

PSALM 35;
JOHN 15:8

Divine rescue op

'... they hid their net for me without cause ...'
(**Psa. 35:7**)

We live in challenging times, in an increasingly secular world where many people reject not only God's very existence and standards for living, but also choose to carve out their own paths and create their own rules.

Consequently, those of us who believe God's Word as truth and seek to apply it to our lives are often regarded as oddities by our non-believing friends and 'soft targets' for all sorts of ridicule, abuse or attack. I remember vividly how, as a young Naval officer serving at sea, some of my male peers and more senior colleagues would try to trip me up at every turn, including making up stories, to undermine me. Whilst undoubtedly I made mistakes along the way, my primary 'offence' was trying to live out what I believed, to the best of my ability, in a very challenging and sometimes seemingly godless environment.

Whilst such experiences are of course painful, as David so clearly expresses in this psalm, we should not be overly surprised or distressed by these things. Jesus told us that the world would hate us in the same way that it hated Him so much that it crucified Him. It is at times like these that we have to make good choices. Some of these, at the heart of this psalm, are trusting and choosing to cry out to the Lord to protect us from these traps; to rescue us when we fall into them; and to vindicate us, knowing that His ways and plans are far greater and better than our own efforts!

Oh Lord, please would You contend with and rescue me from my adversaries. Amen.

DAY 38

PSALM 36;
PHILIPPIANS 4:7

Whilst working as a military doctor, I was called urgently to see a man who was breathing fast, and looked extremely uncomfortable. His face was drawn with anxiety. There were tubes and gowns, raised voices and a multitude of beeps. My heart rate quickened and a hundred questions raced through my mind: First priority? Diagnosis? Treatment? Get more help? I looked at the struggling life before me. Somehow God said to me that what I needed to do, most of all, was to 'meet' this man: to look deep into his eyes and with a peaceful smile, to hold his hand and to be with him in his experience. And so, against my medical training, I followed the prompt.

My colleague marched back into the resuscitation bay and shouted, 'The x-ray shows a massive pneumonia.' Sadly there was no magic medicine at this point. The

Wings of peace

'How priceless is your unfailing love! [People] find refuge in the shadow of your wings.' (Psa. 36:7)

man took a giant sigh, and as a wave of peace gently engulfed him, he accepted that these were his last few minutes. His whole body posture changed, and the anxiety peeled away as he gracefully let go.

Amidst the deep sadness of this event, the thing that struck me was how God bathed both him and me in incredible peace despite everything that was going on. God desires to bring us His unfailing love and peace. If you are feeling sick with stress, or are struggling with buried trauma, ask God to enfold you with the peace that 'passes understanding' right now.

Father I praise You for lavishing Your abundant peace upon us when we face darkness and difficulty – even before we think to ask for it. Amen.

DAY 39

PSALM 37:1–22;
2 CORINTHIANS 4:18

Currently I am living abroad with my husband and enjoying the continental lifestyle. Being in the RAF with overseas allowances, we have a fairly affluent existence, as do all our neighbours. But at the moment I just feel that everyone is trying to 'out do' their neighbour by buying a larger screen TV or getting the 3D version (and making sure we all know about it!) or buying a car with the best tax free deal from the dealership. I find myself getting pulled along by these conversations and I don't like it. Yes, we do actually need a new car but do we need one that will impress 'the Joneses'?

While God graciously promises to give us the desires of our hearts this is not about having a spiritual 'wish list'. I need to be sensible about my motives because He knows even better than I do what is good for me. I know this is true because

Keeping up with 'the Joneses'

'Delight yourself in the LORD and he will give you the desires of your heart. Commit your way to the LORD; trust in him and he will do this.' (Psa. 37:4–5)

sometimes I even find it hard to decide whether something I want is a true desire, or just an item that I fancy having! How many times have I gone shopping and bought something and then never used it? Far too often! We do need certain items to live, but let's try not to get carried away. Our investment in collecting heavenly goods needs to far outweigh the value of any material goods that we can buy here on earth.

Lord, I ask that You look deep inside my heart and help me discern what I should purchase. It is the heavenly goods that I need to store for my salvation, not earthly goods. I trust in You. Amen.

DAY 40

Timekeeper

'Wait for the LORD and keep his way. He will exalt you to inherit the land …' (Psa. 37:34)

Most of us spend a lot of our lives waiting. During my student days I remember at the end of a full day, I would have to wait for the all-elusive London bus and yes, then two or three would turn up at once. We find this frustrating because we believe we are too busy to waste our precious time waiting!

Nowadays, 'I'm late, I'm late for a very important date,' springs to mind. I am rarely on time. It's not good! I need to make more time for jobs and more importantly, for my friends and for God. What about you? Is your quiet time a matter of routine or is it a hurried affair like mine so often is? The psalmist tells us to 'wait for the LORD'. I wish I sat and waited for Him. Perhaps if I did, God would speak more through what I've read or about the situations I am praying about. I know He speaks; I think I am

often just too busy to listen. It takes an effort of will to wait and focus attention on Him, to open my ears and be still. When I do, I find it is the most valuable way I can spend my time. Why not try it yourself for a few days – just sit in silence for a few minutes and ask God to speak to you. If your mind wanders (we are all human) have a notepad and jot down what has come to your mind, then return to God.

Dear Father, I crave a relationship with You. Give me the peace to sit and listen to You. Teach me to wait for You. Amen.

DAY 41

Like David, the writer of this psalm, we've all felt feeble and utterly crushed. As a MoD Contractor, I've often felt that I'm not properly a part of the communities to which I've been posted. I've been treated with suspicion, or kept at arm's length. In contrast, I throw myself headlong into the job, allowing it to rule my life, and to be my identity. Last year I came close to losing my job. It took months of stress before the pressure eased. Bouncing back right away was impossible; I felt so fragile. Then, my military man ended our relationship, which had promised me a purpose outside of work, and a future 'in the club'. Ruined hopes set me back hugely. Past, un-dealt-with bereavement surfaced, and it felt like I had so much to work through, it was hard to know where to start fixing myself.

In Psalm 38 David's depression is

Faith, not feelings!

'O Lord, You know what I long for; you hear all my groans. My heart is pounding, my strength is gone, and my eyes have lost their brightness.'
(Psa. 38:9–10, GNB)

DAY 42

PSALM 39;
MATTHEW 15:18

Overflow!

'I said, "I will watch my ways and keep my tongue from sin; I will put a muzzle on my mouth …"' (Psa. 39:1)

palpable, but he hasn't totally lost hope. He pleads for God to come to his aid, because he still *knows* God is there for him. Many Christians experience very emotional moments in their spiritual journey, but *faith is based on what we know, not how we feel.* Circumstances alter our feelings. We may hit rock bottom. Then, declaring our faith when we definitely don't feel like it is what brings us through.

Father, thank You that faith isn't just for super-spiritual people. Your word says 'God has dealt to each one a measure of faith' (Rom. 12:3, NKJV). Please help me to choose to reassert my faith in You, no matter what my feelings. I praise You that You won't abandon me when I call on You. Amen.

Sometimes I think that I was born with a part of my brain missing – the bit that usually works to make us aware of what we are about to say before we say it! The result of my deficiency is that sometimes other people are amused by what I say, sometimes they are clearly surprised, and sometimes they are hurt. And it all happens so fast that I hadn't planned for or anticipated any of these responses. Jesus rather put His finger on it in Matthew 15 when He said that our words were the overflow of what is already in our hearts … ouch!

The military environment is known for its banter in the workplace, and its gossip on the patch; it is difficult to resist taking part in this, but we all really know deep down that this is not helpful. We need to watch our ways and keep our tongues from sin. We could use this as

a litmus test: What would Jesus think about what I am saying if He was at my shoulder *right now*? And what do my words tell me about what is in my heart?

I pray that God grants me control over my tongue, and transforms my heart. Romans 12:2 describes this process as the 'renewing of [my] mind'. It tells us that we can all try to do this by replacing unhelpful thoughts with God's true Word, the minute we become aware of their presence.

Father God, help me to be aware of what I am saying. Please reveal to me the things that are in my heart, and the things that need to change. Amen.

DAY 43

Out of the mud

'He lifted me out of the slimy pit, out of the mud and mire; he set my feet on a rock and gave me a firm place to stand.' (Psa. 40:2)

When on military exercises, I used to struggle with carrying my kit. At 5'1", my kit weighed nearly half my body-weight, didn't fit properly and was hugely uncomfortable. On patrol, we would get into all-round defensive positions, which usually involved lying somewhere wet and muddy! I would lie there feeling the weight of my Bergen pushing into my aching back and shoulders. I couldn't look up easily as the top of my Bergen would force my head towards the ground. I was desperate to get up as I could cope with the weight when standing. However, standing up was difficult – I always had to be pulled to my feet!

Unfortunately, we all face times where we feel face down in the mud, unable to move due to the weight bearing down us. We struggle to our feet to carry on, only to fall flat on our face again. Friends may help us up, but, when they leave our side, we start to buckle under the weight. Yet there is a way to stand up under the weight. That way is Jesus. If we trust in Him, He will lift us out of the mud and mire and give us a firm place to set our feet. The weight, somehow, becomes more bearable with Jesus holding us up in His arms. He invites anyone who is weary and burdened to come to Him for rest. No weight is too great for Him. He will never let us fall. 'He will not let your foot slip – he who watches over you will not slumber ...' (Psa. 121:3).

Father, help me to take up Your yoke and learn from You. Amen.

DAY 44

We hadn't long moved and I was gradually getting to know the women on the patch. I had started to attend the Women's Bible Study where my faith was being rekindled. Then, one day, God really grabbed my attention! I hadn't felt well when my husband left for work and thought I would rest in bed. By mid-morning I knew something was seriously wrong, but I couldn't get to the phone; it was downstairs and I couldn't stand without severe dizziness. I knew I would fall down the stairs. All I could do was pray in desperation.

A little later, through my open window, I heard a lady from our Bible study group chatting. Later, she said God had told her to walk her dogs at that time, no mean feat as she had three small children and two Alsatians to organise! I crawled to the window and cried for help. Unable to

Answered prayer

get in, they rang my husband who rushed home and called an ambulance. I don't remember anything more until I was woken in hospital by the doctor who had performed emergency life-saving surgery on me. He was wearing an Ichthys badge on his lapel! I made a full recovery.

I don't know why I was taken ill, but I do know that God was looking after me at every stage. Through that experience my faith deepened and my hunger to know more about God was stimulated. I realised just how precious we all are to God and how He really does answer our prayers.

Lord Jesus, thank You that in our suffering, when we cry out to You, You are there for us. Amen.

DAY 45

PSALM 42;
EPHESIANS 1:15–19

Hiding

'Why are you down in the dumps, dear soul? Why are you crying the blues? Fix my eyes on God – soon I'll be praising again. He puts a smile on my face. He's my God.' (Psa. 42:5, *The Message*)

As the wife of a Staff-Sergeant, the three-yearly cycle of our life is Rest, Training, and Tour. That means my husband is not around for two out of three years. During the Training year, he's at home on some weekends, Easter, August, and Christmas holidays. During the Tour year there are fewer weekends and no holidays. His training engrains into him actions essential for his survival, but it's difficult for me to keep calm and carry on. I get the blues, feel sad, and need more hugs on some days.

I think the worst day is the day he leaves for a six-month operational tour. It is unendingly long and heavy, especially as he always seems to leave at 4am. I want to climb back under the duvet, hide my face and cry. Routine helps, until I feel able to turn towards God and fix my eyes on Him, knowing I must do this for my survival;

this is my training ground. As Psalm 42:6 says, it is when I'm lowest, but seeking God, that I learn the things He is teaching me. *When I am in a dark place I must listen only to Him for my soul's survival.* I must diligently train and conscientiously apply myself to His Word and He will show me the course to follow. He doesn't turn away, even when I am slow to listen and develop. Ephesians 1 promises us the riches of His glorious inheritance and the working of His incomparably great power. As we walk in His steps, He will use His creativity and resources through us to reflect His greatness.

Dear Lord, help me to keep my eyes fixed on You especially during the dark days, because You are the source of my light. Amen.

DAY 46

Guidance

**'Send forth your light and your truth,
let them guide me ...' (Psa. 43:3)**

In 1979 I had been praying that God would show me what He wanted me to do with the rest of my life, when I heard a radio advertisement for the Royal Army Educational Corps. I investigated, became more interested, and talked to friends and relatives, who were all very encouraging. I attended the Regular Commissions Board (RCB) still praying that I would know with certainty what God wanted me to do. My Bible study scheme directed me to read Deuteronomy on the first night of RCB and I remember wondering what God could teach me from Deuteronomy!

God soon showed me because I only got as far as Deuteronomy 1:8 when I read the words, 'See I have given you this land. Go in and take possession ...' I suddenly *knew* that I would receive a letter of acceptance and that joining the Army was God's plan for my life. The psalmist asks God to send forth His light and truth so that they can guide him (Psa. 43:3), and it is no different for us today. As we wait on God, immersing ourselves in His light and truth, so we will come into His presence and He will guide us. Even when we are going through tough times and feel downcast (Psa. 43:5), as we put our hope and trust in God, letting Him walk with us and guide us, we can come through into a place of thanks and praise.

Lord, help me to find time to spend with You each day so that I can listen to You speaking to me – guiding me through the good times and the bad. Amen.

DAY 47

When I was away at university, my father and his colleague had business nearby, and planned to visit me. Of course, I had to miss a day's lectures to spruce up my student house. I spent hours on the communal areas that nobody bothered with. I tackled mould on the bathroom ceiling, sweated as I vigorously vacuumed the stairs, hid half-dried laundry, and got the windows gleaming. I was determined that no reports of slovenliness be carried back to my stepmother. Opening the door with my most welcoming smile, my face soon fell. The first thing my dad said was, 'Couldn't you have tidied that up? It looks dreadful lying there,' pointing with his foot to a charity bag on the doorstep. All my effort indoors was worthless; judgment had already been passed.

What I couldn't do was shout back in protest, but in Psalm 44, God's people

DAY 48

It's OK to shout!

'Wake up, O Lord! Why do you sleep?
Get up! Do not reject us forever.'
(Psa. 44:23, NLT)

shout at their heavenly Father. Despite their best efforts and their faithfulness to His ways, they're in a situation where they're oppressed and disgraced. They feel they've done everything right, but God isn't seeing it. They're still suffering. God doesn't get cross when we yell at Him – He's big enough to take us venting our emotions when we feel unjustly treated, or we need His help more quickly than it seems to be coming. Opening up to Him and being real is how we develop a closer relationship, and God longs for that with us.

Thank You, Lord, that You want to hear from me when I'm angry and upset, and when I question You. Help me to trust that You will rescue me because of Your unfailing love. Amen.

You are beautiful!

'The king is enthralled by your beauty;
honour him, for he is your lord.'
(Psa. 45:11)

The nature of Service life is such that it can be easy to lose sight of our true identity, in particular how the Lord looks upon each one of us as the wonderfully created and fantastically beautiful bride of Christ with whom He plans to spend eternity.

I was a young officer shortly after women started to serve on board warships at sea, and I remember vividly being issued with ill-fitting men's uniform during the changeover period. It is difficult to feel beautiful when you are wearing gym shorts which are eight inches too big around your waist in order to get them over your hips; when you are driving the ship's small boat in white tropical uniform after the heavens have seemingly poured out their full water content upon you such that your uniform is now even more transparent than was previously the case; or when you are on exercise on a damp, windy moor, in combat fatigues, looking somewhat bedraggled and tired after another night of keeping watch for potential 'enemies'!

Whilst such experiences are an integral aspect of Service life (where a keen sense of humour is often key to surviving and perhaps even enjoying them!), it is important that they do not influence or change our perspectives of *who we really are*. As the verse in Isaiah makes clear, the Lord clothes us with His very nature, not least His salvation and righteousness. They are such precious and beautiful jewels in His sight that He is enthralled by our beauty.

Dear Lord, please help me to better understand and perceive how You regard me, especially on those days when I don't feel beautiful. Amen.

DAY 49

PSALM 46;
DEUTERONOMY 31:1–8

Our refuge and strength

**'God is our refuge and strength, an
ever-present help in trouble.' (Psa. 46:1)**

Whatever we are going through, our heavenly Father knows all about it and will guide us through the difficult times. My father was in the Army and I remember the times when he was away on exercise or overseas for weeks on end. My mother provided the stability for all four children and we were just so excited when our daddy came home.

God knows how hard it is to be alone, whether we are keeping the home fires burning, or away serving Him in a foreign land. God's words to Joshua are just as relevant to us today, 'The LORD himself goes before you and will be with you; He will never leave you nor forsake you. Do not be afraid; do not be discouraged' (Deut. 31:8). Similarly, in Psalm 46 we read the promise that our loving heavenly Father will always be there for us. He will see us through difficult and lonely times. He will protect each of us and supply our needs. We can go to Him at any time for the strength we need. *The God who rules over His creation cares about each one of us and wants the best for us.* Isn't that wonderful? If we can see that our Lord is with us in the dark times, how we can rejoice when the light comes! We are encouraged to be still in God's presence and to soak up His love. He longs to hold us close in His arms. There really is no safer place to be.

Thank You, Lord, that we can run into the safety of Your loving arms and find unconditional love and protection there. Amen.

DAY 50

PSALM 47;
LUKE 6:23

My children's granddad isn't given to great outbursts but every now and again they will persuade him to put on a silly voice and shout 'Yippee!' Then everyone falls about laughing. How many times have we shouted 'Yippee' just because we can? Too often (especially in the Military) we dwell on the bad things that are happening and these are the things we talk to God about.

Psalm 47 is a song of praise, an overflowing of feeling good; verse 1 says, 'Clap your hands … shout to God with cries of joy.' Jesus loved to be among people spreading joy. Being with Him must have been a bit like being at a party. In fact, Jesus' first miracle was at a wedding banquet. He enjoyed having a good time!

When was the last time you really laughed? Laughing is very therapeutic

DAY 51

Yippee!

'God has ascended amid shouts of joy ...' (Psa. 47:5)

and, as it uses a lot of muscles, it is also good for keeping fit! I sometimes feel guilty if I'm really happy and just enjoying myself. And yet, as I look around me, there are loads of things to feel happy about. I have a good roof over my head, I have food in the cupboard, I have two wonderful children, I have some very good friends – I have lots of things to make me happy. What do you have that makes you happy? What things make you laugh? Why not make a bit of time in your day to sing praises to God then let yourself go and laugh just because you can – I bet Jesus joins in with you!

Thank You, Lord, for Your gift of guilt-free laughter. Amen.

PSALM 48;
HEBREWS 10:25

Psalm 48 is a great song of praise to God, attributed to 'the sons of Korah', who were the worship leaders of the day during David's time. Communal worship in the Temple was a duty of the Israelites, and in New Testament times the writer to the Hebrews exhorted his readers not to give up this practice. I did my teaching practice in Llangollen, and met some lovely Christian folk at the non-Conformist chapel in the town while I was there. Some years later I returned to Llangollen and called unexpectedly on my friends. They made me very welcome and we had a hilarious evening talking about 'entertaining angels without knowing it' (Heb. 13:2).

We likened being a Christian to being a three-pin plug: fairly useless unless you are connected to an electrical socket whereby you can be a conduit of power.

Get plugged in

'Within your temple, O God, we meditate on your unfailing love.' (Psa. 48:9)

We are also like lumps of coal; each lump is kept burning, giving off light and heat, whilst in the fire with other coals, but it soon becomes much less effective when removed from the rest of the coals. No wonder the sons of Korah exhorted the Israelites to give praise to God for His greatness, to remember His deeds, to meet in the Temple, meditate on His Word, and to tell the next generation. It is sometimes difficult in Service life to find other Christians, but it is vital that we search them out, meet together, encourage one another and spur each other on in our Christian lives.

Forgive me, Lord, when I neglect to meet with other Christians. Help me to make meeting with others a priority. Amen.

DAY 52

PSALM 49;
MATTHEW 13:1–9,8–23

Sowing seeds

**'But God will redeem my life from the grave;
he will surely take me to himself.'
(Psa. 49:15)**

When I was deployed to Macedonia in 1999, I was straight out of training and knew almost nothing about real life in the Army. It was a big step into the unknown, and quite a daunting prospect. To begin with, we slept in a disused factory, everyone lying side-by-side in their sleeping bags. It was cold, with snow on the ground outside. At night, I used to read my Bible before I went to sleep. Living in such close proximity makes you quickly aware of everyone's habits, both good and bad!

My Sergeant Major noticed what I was reading, and throughout the six months we had some amazing conversations about God and faith. On one recce there was the most incredible sunset and he could see the creative hand of God at work, in contrast to the pain and devastation that man had caused around us. He asked me many searching questions wanting to understand how God could allow the suffering we witnessed. I struggled to answer these questions in words, but prayed that the 'utterance from my heart [would] give understanding' (Psa. 49:3).

This psalm paints a bleak picture of death without God, but God offers hope as He redeems our lives from the grave, despite the grief and the pain. These were the seeds I tried to sow, but only God knows where they fell. Many of us feel our words are clumsy and inadequate (and they are!) but God *still* uses us to sow His seeds.

Father, help me to find ways of showing Your love to the world, and grant me boldness as I attempt to carry them out. Amen.

DAY 53

PSALM 50;
MATTHEW 10:29–31

Most military bases are located in the middle of the countryside so there is usually plenty of wildlife to be spotted. Whilst travelling between two RAF units on the way to work, I noticed a sick wild rabbit sitting at the side of the road. Over the weekend I couldn't get this picture out of my head so I purposely drove back to the place I last saw it in the hope of finding him and helping him. I soon found this starving, bulging-eyed sorry sight. I picked him up and took him to the vet where they confirmed he was suffering from myxomatosis. Sadly he had to be put to sleep but I knew this was better than him dying in agony at the side of the road.

This experience made me consider how God's eyes are on the whole of His creation and nothing is out of His sight. Whether you feel isolated, lonely, misunderstood, insecure, afraid, rejected,

God is in control

**'I know every bird in the mountains …'
(Psa. 50:11)**

depressed, sick, or are suffering alone or far from your loved ones, *God's eyes are on you.* As Jesus says, God cares when a sparrow dies; He numbers the very hairs on our heads. He says we are 'worth more than many sparrows' (Matt. 10:31). *Wow!* God's sovereignty extends even to a bird (or rabbit) dying. So do not worry. Whatever you are going through, your heavenly Father knows all about it.

Father, please help me to trust that You are sovereign in all situations. Nothing that has happened, is happening or will happen to me is out of Your control, or beyond Your sight. Thank You that You care for me. Amen.

DAY 54

PSALM 51;
1 PETER 2:9–10

I had not been in the Army long when I made what I felt was a significant error of judgment. I felt very guilty and was tempted to deny the incident or blame someone else. Eventually I took the situation to God in prayer and knew I needed to own up to my mistake. I took a deep breath and went to my OC to admit to what had happened. The OC was very understanding and forgiving, and immediately I felt God's peace flood into my heart.

David, the psalmist, felt a long way from God. In his case, he had had an affair with Bathsheba and arranged for her husband to be killed in battle. Following a visit from Nathan the prophet, he was racked with guilt and in Psalm 51 he admits his sin (vv.1–4), asks for forgiveness (vv.7–9) and repents (vv.10–12). Notice that he was forgiven.

Out of the darkness

'Have mercy on me, O God, according to your unfailing love; according to your great compassion …' (Psa. 51:1)

Jesus' genealogy in Matthew 1:6 shows that Solomon, son of Bathsheba, was in his direct family tree.

So if you are in a dark place, examine your life before God and confess and repent of any sin that He shows you. But do not let Satan accuse you falsely. Do not navel-gaze, but fix your eyes on the beautiful face of Jesus, your Saviour and Redeemer. Rest in His truth and let Him walk through the dark places with you.

Thank You, Jesus, that You bore my sin on the cross and that You know what it is like to be in a dark place. Please help me to know Your presence with me whatever my circumstances. Amen.

DAY 55

PSALM 52;
HEBREWS 6:19

Who holds your future?

'... in your name I will hope,
for your name is good.' (Psa. 52:9)

DAY 56

PSALM 53;
1 PETER 5:7

Have you ever prayed to God 'in hope' for something? Hope for the right posting, the right school, the right job, perhaps? It can sometimes feel that we pray with our fingers crossed. 'Please God, if we could just have that posting at that time, then everything will be OK.' I'm really good at looking to the future, deciding which course of action would be best and then asking God to bless my excellent plan and make it come to pass! I'm advising the God who hung the stars in place and who knows the end from the beginning.

Put like that it sounds more than faintly ridiculous. While we are busy mapping out our own future, we often neglect to discover God's perfect plan, so carefully and lovingly crafted (Jer. 29:11). And – breaking news – He has no desire to keep the plan secret, because He wants us to live it!

We talk about hope in a wishful-thinking kind of way, but God isn't a genie we can conjure out of a lamp. God wants more than anything for us to experience His love and to walk in His ways. I most often want the best *and* an easy and comfortable life. The two aren't always the same! God's plan for us is better than any of our own ideas. Praise God that we can put our hope in Him knowing that our souls can rest firmly and securely, *whatever our future may hold.*

Lord, I know that Your plans for my life are perfect. Help me to trust my future to You, knowing that You love me without measure and for eternity. Amen.

As a Troop Commander I had a fantastic opportunity to do some surveying in French-speaking Africa. I was so excited, especially at the prospect of going to countries that I'd not even heard of before, like Togo and Benin.

The reality, however, was far from my dreams. Two of my soldiers were caught in a civil war in Guinea-Bissau. Thankfully, after three days of shelling, they were rescued by the Senegalese Navy. We had been seriously concerned for their lives. In that incident we lost over half a million pounds' worth of equipment and I had to travel back to the UK to justify borrowing additional survey equipment in order to carry out work in Madagascar.

All seemed to be going much better and I sent two more guys into bandit country to survey the roads, whilst I stayed in the capital with another soldier,

Fearing the worst

'There they were, overwhelmed with dread, where there was nothing to dread.' (Psa. 53:5)

Headstrong or strong head?

'Surely God is my help; the Lord is the one who sustains me.' (Psa. 54:4)

manning two base stations. We'd had daily communications with the other team for three days and then nothing. Simultaneously, the government authority accused us of spying and threatened to confiscate our equipment and imprison us if we didn't stop surveying within twenty-four hours and leave the country soon afterwards. Fearing the worst, I requested a police search for the soldiers. Just in time, they returned safely, explaining that the satellite phone had broken and furious that I hadn't trusted them to finish the survey!

Lord, I'm sorry for the times when I've failed to bring my worries to You daily, and they have built up and filled me with fear and dread. Help me to not be anxious about anything but to remember that You care for me. Amen.

As an Army officer of some experience I'm reasonably competent and don't like it when others try to tell me how to do my job. I'm even worse when it comes to comment or criticism in my role as a mother, especially if it comes from my own mother! Sometimes I even get cross when God appears not to be working to my plan or timelines for a situation and, I confess, I resist His plan!

Having just stopped work for maternity leave, I have been amazed in the last week how my little baby is so dependent upon us for everything, even supporting her head and adjusting her position. Mostly she is compliant and looks to us for provision of absolutely everything. However, sometimes she also has a stubborn streak, arching her back and thrashing her head around – often causing her to head-butt something as she resists our help! It has

made me understand better how God must delight when we depend on Him and continually seek His guidance to do His will; but also how He must watch with disappointment and amazement as we struggle to do things on our own, ignoring Him. What rational thinking can ever allow us to think that we can do things better than the Creator of the universe? Let us give up on our worldly pride and yield to the Father who loves us and has good and perfect plans for us.

Almighty God, Lord over all creation, I'm sorry for the times when I try to do things my way. Help me to depend on You more fully and to seek Your will, Your way and Your timing. Amen.

DAY 58

PSALM 55;
LUKE 22:1–6,47

Betrayed!

**'I said, "Oh, that I had the wings of a dove!
I would fly away and be at rest – I would flee
far away and stay in the desert ..."'**
(Psa. 55:6–7)

During my first weekend in Afghanistan, I went on a foot patrol around the villages on the outskirts of Kabul. The landscape was arid and dry. Nothing could possibly grow there. We came across an apparently deserted village and I remember asking the Patrol Commander if this village had been bombed as it was in such a rundown state. He said that this was what all the villages were like. I remember wondering how anyone could survive life in such a hostile environment.

An even more hostile environment, however, can be our own emotions after betrayal by a close friend. In today's psalm, David is wracked by exactly this type of searing pain. What makes it worse for him is that this friend was someone with whom he shared everything including faith (v.14). He longs to flee the situation, preferring even the desert to the anguish of heart he currently faces. There truly is no pain that cuts as deeply as betrayal; one wife I know whose husband left her for another woman admitted that there were days when she wished he had died as it would have been easier to cope with the separation and severing of love through death than it was through the pain of his treachery. Jesus too knew the terrible betrayal of a friend when Judas, one of his 'inner circle' sold him for 30 pieces of silver.

Perhaps you are experiencing pain of betrayal. Bring it before God safe in the knowledge that He understands exactly what you are going through and He is full of compassion and unending love towards you.

Father, please sustain me in my pain and heal my sorrow. Amen.

DAY 59

PSALM 56;
JOHN 14:26–27

When my husband went to Afghanistan I really wanted to show the community where I was living that I could cope on my own and that God's amazing love would uphold me through anything. It didn't work out the way I had planned, however, and within two weeks of the tour starting, I was feeling alone and afraid as I drove our precious little girl to A&E with all the symptoms of meningitis. The doctors weren't able to give a firm diagnosis so they sent us home telling me to wake her every hour during the night and, if she didn't respond, to call for an ambulance. It was the longest night ever. I had to draw on God's strength just to get me through. I was *so* afraid.

Reflecting on the whole episode, I realised I wanted to show off God to my friends, to show how *He* would sustain me through anything and how wonderful He

He sustains

'When I am afraid, I will trust in you. In God, whose word I praise, in God I trust; I will not be afraid.' (Psa. 56:3–4)

is. He did and He is – but, the problem was, I was trying to do it in my own strength. He allowed me to be humbled until I fell on my knees in a desperate and frightened prayer. I really had to draw closer to Him to keep going.

God will be exalted by who you are and what you do; don't make my mistake and try to exalt Him yourself. Draw closer to Him in everything you do and take any opportunity to pray.

DAY 60

PSALM 57;
PHILIPPIANS 3:1

Music at dawn is an acquired taste! The sound of my daughter playing the violin before school was certainly enough to 'awaken the dawn', and probably the next door neighbours too! Shortly after being posted to Germany I remember being woken by the sound of a brass band. The noise went on sufficiently long enough for me to get dressed and go and investigate. I discovered a *Schutzenfest* (shooting festival) parade with costumed hunters, drum majorettes and at least five uniformed bands. The jolly music being played was rather different in character to the military bands which I have seen at various regimental parades, and whose stirring beat inspire me to imagine long ago battles where soldiers marched to war with pipes and drums.

Music can really affect our emotions, and Psalm 57, set to the tune 'Do Not

Dawn chorus

'Awake, my soul! Awake, harp and lyre! I will awaken the dawn.' (Psa. 57:8)

Destroy,' is a soldier's song. Despite being written after a retreat it encourages the singer to press on, to remain steadfast and hold tight to God's faithfulness. Many times in my own life pressing forward after a setback is hard; what I really want to do is find a quiet hole to lie in and lick my wounds. It is times like these that I most need the support of a church fellowship (even an early morning church fellowship!) and the encouragement to my spirit that singing stirring hymns of praise to God with others often brings. Paul writes that rejoicing in the Lord is a 'safeguard' to us.

Father God, thank You for the gift of music to stir my spirit to worship You, even in the face of defeat. Amen.

DAY 61

God as Judge

'... surely there is a God who judges
the earth.' (Psa. 58:11)

Often, when I have been sharing the good news of Jesus Christ with military personnel, I've been met with misunderstanding about the nature and character of God. Most people have heard He is loving but don't appreciate He is a *God of justice* too. Yes, out of love, God sent His Son Jesus Christ into the world to die for our sins. But Jesus died for our sins to satisfy the justice of God by paying the punishment for those sins so we wouldn't have to. When I was a dog handler in the RAF I used to think about God as I patrolled the base at night. If I had to shoot someone or release my dog, what would God think? I'm sure many of us in the Military ask ourselves these kinds of questions.

Interestingly, it wasn't God's love but the prospect of His judgment that eventually bought me to a place of repentance as I trusted Jesus Christ for my forgiveness and salvation. Once I finally understood what Jesus had done for me, the fear of facing God left me. One day we will all stand before God to give an account of our lives. At the final judgment those who have trusted Christ are safe in God's hands. How awful for those who reject the love and justice of God and have to face punishment for their sins. Today, in prayer, why not come before the living God who loves you and receive His forgiveness with thanksgiving, perhaps for the first time.

Father, You are a God of love and justice.
Please help me to place my trust in You for
Your forgiveness and mercy. Amen.

DAY 62

And the prince kissed the princess and they lived happily ever after ...

Only, my life wasn't a fairy tale and I discovered I wasn't a princess and he certainly wasn't a prince! There wasn't any happy ever after. At first, it *was* like a fairy tale. The vows 'to love and to cherish, to have and to hold' were a comfort, but then life got in the way and the arguments started and I didn't know if that was better or worse than the strained silences. I just wanted to scream and release all my pent-up emotions. It was hard to know who to turn to; I didn't want to bother my friends with it all.

Even though I felt all alone and there seemed no one to talk to, God knew. He saw what I was going through, every cold look, every harsh word and every bit of pain. In the words of this psalm, He was my 'strength', going 'before me',

Happily ever after?

'But I will sing of your strength, in the morning I will sing of your love; for you are my fortress, my refuge in times of trouble.' (Psa. 59:16)

surrounding me with His presence 'like a shield' (Psa. 59:9–11). I discovered that He was my fortress in times of trouble and that He loved me. Paul writes of the wonderful hope we have when the eyes of our hearts are 'enlightened' (Eph. 1:18). I needed God to open my eyes to see that even though the 'happily ever after' had been lost, I still had a glorious inheritance in Him. This hope is freely available to all of us, *whatever* we are going through. He longs for us to pour out our hearts to Him and see Him as the prince we've always dreamed of!

Take time to pour out to God what is in your heart today.

DAY 63

PSALM 60;
ROMANS 12:12

Recently my pilot husband went away on a trip with work. That should be no great hardship, the nature of his work means that he frequently goes away for short periods of time. This time, however, he went just as we had many things we needed to be doing together; a project at church was looming on top of an inordinate amount to do around the house and an endless list of phone calls and emails. Even better (!) the aircraft then broke down and thus extended the trip significantly. So, what did I do? *Exactly* what the psalmist did here. I complained! I ranted about how much work I had to do and how everything was always left to me and how difficult my life is when he is not there. I assumed God had forgotten about me.

After a while, I came to realise that it was I who had forgotten about Him.

Be prayerful

'You have rejected us, O God, and burst forth upon us; you have been angry – now restore us!' (Psa. 60:1)

How easy it is when things get difficult to put our heads down and charge on through, feeling that there is no one to help. That is why I love the second part of verse 1, 'now restore us'. In this case it was my anger with God that was getting in the way of our relationship, but the solution is always the same, He longs for us to turn to Him and receive His love again and again and again.

Lord, I know You love me and want the best for me. Help me not to assume You have given me the worst but to seek Your guidance in the difficult times. Thank You that You care so much for me. Amen.

DAY 64

Beyond the wire

'I long to dwell in your tent forever and take refuge in the shelter of your wings.'
(Psa. 61:4)

DAY 65

We were moving to another MQ and, for the first time in our married life, we would be living inside camp, 'behind the wire'. I really wasn't looking forward to it as it gave me the feeling of being hemmed in. It was also more difficult to invite people to 'drop in for a coffee and a chat' as they had to be booked in at the guardroom and it felt isolated from the local community. To make things worse, we were situated right at the edge of camp and thus the view from our house was of the wire.

We soon discovered, however, that the view beyond the wire was over open fields and we spent many hours with our young son watching the wildlife, the crops grow, the tractors and combine harvesters work the field, or just admiring the view of the countryside. We also found that due to the reduced road-traffic and the security

of the camp, it was great for the older children to have some independence whilst still being protected. Sometimes we see the protection and guidelines given to us by God as a constraint, to hem us in and ruin our fun, but when we are in trouble, and as we trust Him more, we see His guidelines as our safe boundaries and His wings as our shelter.

Lord, thank You that You care for us. Thank You for Your protection and wisdom. Help me to see beyond the boundaries to the freedoms that You give me as I trust in You and Your love more each day. Amen.

I never wanted to be married to a clergyman or anyone in the Armed Forces but here I am with both! The readings today are about trusting God's will for our lives, *even when it is contrary to our expectations*. David, who wrote this psalm, experienced God's constant hand over his life even when he ended up in places he didn't want to be. It's there that we see him declaring his rock-solid faith in God *alone*. He was able to do this because he acknowledged who God was and recalled God's faithfulness in the past. Sometimes the challenges of military life become too much for me to bear ... until I look to God and remember His faithfulness over the years.

Look back over your life. Remember how God has been faithful to *you*. Ask Him to allow you to see the past and the present through His eyes and not with

In God alone

'Trust in him at all times, O people; pour out your hearts to him, for God is our refuge.' (Psa. 62:8)

your own understanding. He alone knows each of our situations and loves us so completely that He can be trusted to see us through. Whether it be dealing with a deployment, struggling to make new friends, fearing change or coping as a temporary single parent, hang in there; David did this and God didn't fail him. Neither will God fail you.

Faithful God, thank You for always being there for me; please will You instil in me the conviction that You will still be there for me in the future and I can trust in You alone. When I am tempted to rely on myself or others, remind me that only Your way is best. Amen.

DAY 66

PSALM 63;
SONG OF SOLOMON 2:4

The further along I go in my journey of faith, the more I've come to see that it is in the times of difficulty, times when I cry out to God in desperation, that I truly see His glory and love for me. Two years in Catterick felt dry and barren! At that time it seemed like there was little in the way of Christian friendship and fellowship. I often felt spiritually parched and empty. Like all seasoned military wives, I am very proficient at clicking into my 'default setting', which is to get busy. I feared being alone and was trying to avoid it. However, this tactic left me feeling burnt out and my faith began to perish. Just then God spoke to me through a book I was reading and I came to realise that He was asking me to *rest* in His sanctuary, rather than *rush around*.

In the first two verses of this psalm we see that David is thirsty and weary but,

Sanctuary

'I have seen you in the sanctuary and beheld your power and your glory.' (Psa. 63:2)

as he gazes upon the power and glory of God, he is revived. We also see that when David takes his eye off the barrenness of his situation and enters into God's sanctuary, his soul becomes satisfied as though he has eaten the finest, choicest foods (Psa. 63:5). As I discovered in the busyness of life, finding our sanctuary can be tough, but, if we purposefully seek this special place, there is a banquet waiting.

Lord Jesus, thank You that You provide a sanctuary for me, an oasis where I can find Your life-giving water. Please help me to turn to Your dwelling place when I am parched and hungry. Amen.

Words that wound

'**They sharpen their tongues like swords,
and aim cruel words like arrows.**'
(Psa. 64:3, GNB)

I don't know who came up with the proverb, 'Sticks and stones can break our bones, but words can never hurt us', but in my experience it is not true. At least bones mend in time, whereas hurtful words can lodge in our hearts and continue to cause pain for years afterwards.

In training at Sandhurst we were continually bombarded by verbal attacks from the staff, to see how we would react under pressure. One of my friends, whose surname is Hall, was relieved that the tirades were being directed at someone called Hill. He confessed that he would have given up if he'd received that level of criticism. It was only later that he discovered there was no Hill; the staff had got the name wrong and the insults were actually intended for him!

Do you have words lodged like an arrow in your heart? Are you still hurt or wounded long after the event? Jesus doesn't want us to continue to carry such burdens. They can lead to us bearing grudges and holding resentment. We nurse our wounds, justify our actions and rehearse the incident, while healing and restoration are what Jesus wants for us. He wants to set us free from our self-made prisons and experience His complete freedom. Hear again those words of Jesus 'Love your enemies and pray for those who persecute you' (Matt. 5:44).

Father, I come to You because others have hurt and wounded me with their words. Help me to forgive them and to be restored in my relationship with them. I ask that You would bless them today because they are also broken people. Amen.

I often ask myself: why is it that God appears to answer some prayers and not others? I've heard a number of preachers assert that God always answers prayers and He has three stock answers: 'Yes', 'No' and 'Wait'! And here, the psalmist assures us that God *does* hear and answer our prayers.

I have been a Christian for over fifty years and on many occasions I've been disappointed that God has not answered my prayers in the way that I would have chosen. Looking back I can see that, as I have come before God in prayer over a particular situation, committed the circumstances to Him and asked for His Sovereign will to be done, so He has been able to put His plan for my life into operation. Take my request for a particular posting, for example. I didn't get the posting that I wanted, yet the posting that I was given was a fantastic

DAY 69

Answered prayer

'O you who hear prayer, to you all men will come.' (Psa. 65:2)

preparation for future tours and resulted both in my being posted to Shrivenham (where I met my husband) and, later, in promotion.

Having now retired from the Army I am in a privileged position in the Armed Forces' Christian Union office as part of a prayer union that prays for many individuals and situations. I can bear testimony to amazing answers to prayer and assert with the psalmist that God does indeed 'answer us with awesome deeds of righteousness' (v.5), and that, as our cross reference for today says, '… in all things God works for the good of those who love him' (Rom. 8:28).

Thank You, Lord, that You always answer prayer in our best interests. May Your will be done in my life. Amen.

The furnace of adversity

'For you, O God, tested us; you refined us like silver.' (Psa. 66:10)

As I read about God's faithfulness to His people after they left Egypt and went into the desert, my thoughts turn to another desert where my husband is currently serving for six months. His descriptions are full of the all-pervading dust, heat and bareness of the desert. It is an inhospitable and hostile terrain. There have been a few times in my life where it has felt as if I have wandered into a metaphorical desert. I remember a posting to Bergen-Hohne (Germany) where God used adversity to strip away all the things that insulated me from really knowing myself. God often seemed absent, my prayers felt powerless and it seemed that everything fell apart. I wondered why God was allowing this, assuming (mistakenly) that I was being punished for some unknown failing.

You can imagine how comforted I was to learn that many of the great saints experienced time in the desert *just before* the glorious fulfilment of the promises God had made to them. Even Jesus had time in the desert. God can use the desert to prepare, consecrate and refine our character. The psalmist describes God like a silversmith heating up silver-ore over a furnace. As the heat increases so all the dross rises to the surface, ready to be scooped off. Long ago, a silversmith would know the silver was finally pure when his own face was reflected on its molten surface. Just so, God seeks to purify us through desert experiences so that we can mirror His image to the world.

Lord, please use my trials and times in the desert so that I am refined like silver and Your image is reflected in my character. Amen.

DAY 70

A great harvest

**'Then the land will yield its harvest ...'
(Psa. 67:6)**

I came across verse 6 during a two-month period without rain. I had been praying for rain as my horses were finding very little grass in the paddock, at a time when it should have been lush and green. I knew that would mean a poor hay harvest and it struck me how many times in the Bible God promises good harvests to the nation that fears Him, is obedient to Him and praises Him. It drove me to pray for our nation, to ask God's forgiveness for our waywardness and to ask Him to bring revival to our churches and people. I praised God a few days later when we had about twenty hours of continuous, soft rain that sank deep into the ground and turned the grass green again. What a bounteous God who blesses us despite our unworthiness!

Jesus told His disciples to go out and preach the gospel, making disciples of all nations. He also said that the '[fields] are ripe for harvest' (John 4:35). I hear of the spiritual hunger amongst our Service personnel and their families and know that revival will only come with much prayer and all of us Christians (not just the chaplains) seeking opportunities to lead others to Jesus and then discipling them. How wonderful if it were our military community that led our nation back to God! Then we would truly see God blessing our nation and the land yielding its harvest.

Lord, I'm sorry that so often I fail to share the good news of You with others. Inspire me to think and act and speak for You. Amen.

DAY 71

Have you ever moved to a new posting and had no one come to knock on your door or invite you round for coffee? You're not the only one! It can be a very lonely life constantly moving and settling into new locations as a military spouse – not knowing anyone in the community, or how to find the supermarket or the contact for the local Beaver group. And what about the trauma of finding another hairdresser?! But how wonderful it is when someone does make the effort to be friendly and include you in what's going on.

One of the joys for me of being a Christian is having a ready-made 'family' wherever I go, often found in my local church; people who will encourage my husband, my children and myself, pray for us or simply offer us a cup of coffee and a listening ear. The best postings that I have experienced have been those with

Coffee, anyone?

**'God sets the lonely in families ...'
(Psa. 68:6)**

not only welcoming churches, but where I have also had supportive Bible study, fellowship groups and even prayer triplets. Perhaps none of those exist where you are now. Pray that God will provide someone with whom you could meet regularly to pray or to study the Bible. Look out too for those who are new in your congregation that you might be the one to offer words of encouragement and support.

Lord, thank You that You provide other believers to be 'family' when I am far from my own. Show me how I might be 'family' to those around me who are new or lonely so that we can all know the joy of fellowship with You. Amen.

DAY 72

PSALM 68:18–35;
ZEPHANIAH 3:17

What kind of response have you had from non-Christians when they find out you're a Christian? I have had two standard responses in five years with the RAF: shock and a loss for words, or an immediate recall of the last time they were in church! Too often I am disheartened and disappointed by my own response to those moments. Why don't I seize these opportunities to share my love and passion for God? I find plenty of excuses not to. I feel intimidated or unsure, or fear that I may sound plain silly. Afterwards I remember that God wants to speak through me and *all I have to be is willing*. He has the words that can touch someone's heart and I need to trust Him more to do just that.

I think of the times that I have been overwhelmed by the simplicity of the gospel. The amazing words of the psalmist

The simple truth

**'Our God is a God who saves;
from the Sovereign LORD comes
escape from death.' (Psa. 68:20)**

show that he understands this. Our God saves.

Zephaniah 3:17 says 'He will take great delight in you ...' We have a God who loves us so much that He delights in us. We don't need to share the technicalities of being a Christian; instead we need to share the passionate love that He has for us and we have for Him. *That* is the explanation for why we have this faith. The rest shines through that love. Let's be challenged to tell the world more about our God who saves *because He loves*.

Father, You are the God who saves. Thank You for what You have done in our lives. Help us to share You more with the people we meet. Amen.

DAY 73

PSALM 69:1–18;
ROMANS 8:37–39

Certainty

'... answer me with your sure salvation.'
(Psa. 69:13)

The salvation of Jesus Christ is the most precious gift in the world and there is nothing better when you go through trials than for God to remind you that you are still His. When I was struggling with ill-health, a broken heart and facing having to leave my role as an evangelist within the Military, I cried out to God. I asked Him to reassure me that I still belonged to Him. He gave me a verse that reminded me of His faithfulness and left me without doubt that I was still His.

As Christians we walk by faith and not by sight so, when tough times come, we need reassurance that God is still with us, cares for us and is faithful to His promises. That encouragement can come in many ways, through Scripture, the kindness of people, the testimony of other Christians and the prayers of God's people.

This psalm deals with a common experience in the Christian walk, 'My eyes fail, looking for my God' (Psa. 69:3). When the hard times come, it can seem like we can't see God in the situation, but even when we don't see Him or can't seem to hear His voice, He is *still* by our side. We will experience all sorts of hardships in this world but that's why Romans 8 is so helpful. Even when we don't 'feel' loved by God those verses remind us that '[nothing] will be able to separate us from the love of God that is in Christ Jesus our Lord' (Rom. 8:39).

Lord, when I go through trials, please remind me of Your love and reassure me of Your salvation. Amen.

DAY 74

PSALM 69:19–36;
PROVERBS 18:24

Where are your friends when you need them? Invariably, I find they are always around when I am busy and wanting to get on, but where are they when I *really* need someone to talk to? For instance, when I get a phone call from my husband or child at school and they are having a hard time, naturally I get worried! From past experience, they are probably feeling a lot better now that they have unloaded it all onto me – but who can *I* unload it onto? Or, there are times when I've done something really stupid. We all do things and get into situations we shouldn't because we are lonely or scared, but where do we turn, when we realise the enormity of our mistakes in the cold light of day? Who is there, with the time, *just for us*?

It appears that in Psalm 69 the writer's heart has been broken and he has been left helpless: 'I looked for sympathy, but

When I needed a neighbour

'I looked in vain for one friendly face. Not one. I couldn't find one shoulder to cry on.' (Psa. 69:20, *The Message*)

there was none, for comforters, but I found none' (Psa. 69:20). And yet, by the end of the psalm, he is praising God. Why? Verse 33 says 'The LORD hears the needy and does not despise His captive people.' *God* is waiting for you. There is nothing you could have done that will shock Him and nothing too small that He wouldn't want to hear about it. He is the best friend ever. He is never too busy. It's never too late and the love and peace you can find in Him are indescribable!

Pause. Spend time today being totally honest with God and giving Him all your worries.

DAY 75

PSALM 70;
JOHN 6:40

It all seemed so exciting getting married to a RAF Fast Jet pilot and settling into our first quarter in a Fast Jet Station. Exciting – that is – until the first glimpse of what life might be like, a few short weeks later! My parents were coming to stay and a quick flying trip was programmed for my new husband that Sunday. 'No worries,' he said, 'I'll be back early afternoon ...' Two days later he returned, having taken off and been unable to return because of fog! And so the pattern continued throughout his flying career with delays caused by the weather, or the un-serviceability of the aircraft, or some other reason.

It's easy to rejoice in God when things are going well. But not so easy when the children are tired, you feel tetchy, or ill, and the washing machine has packed up. You hang on for the hour when he's going

When the going gets tough …

'… may those who love your salvation always say, "Let God be exalted!"' (Psa. 70:4)

to walk through the door and take over, but then the phone rings and he tells you of yet another delay. We may even wonder 'What's the point of being a Christian?' It *can* feel it is not working out the way it should. Just so, the psalmist David often felt his life was one catastrophe after another. Despite this, he still made a point of praising God for the good things He had done in the past. Whatever you are going through right now, remember to give praise to God for the free gift of salvation that He offers to us through Christ; the greatest gift of all!

Thank You, God, that however tough life sometimes feels, I can still give You praise that I have been made whole through Christ. Amen.

DAY 76

PSALM 71;
LAMENTATIONS 3:22–23

Growing in Him

'Since my youth, O God, you have taught me, and to this day I declare your marvellous deeds.' (Psa. 71:17)

DAY 77

PSALM 72;
ISAIAH 61:1

I can remember clearly those early days of marriage to a RAF officer and being somewhat in awe of the senior officers' wives living in their large houses. I am now well past the age that they were and, unsurprisingly, don't feel quite as old as they once seemed! My hair has been grey for many years and yet I am still praising God. It is great to look back over the years and to see God's continual hand on our lives. Those postings that I couldn't understand at the time, I now see as God teaching me and refining me and I can even see where, incredibly, He used me to achieve His purposes. His paths have not necessarily been the ones that I would have chosen but they are the ones that have deepened my faith and helped me to understand His character more.

We can praise God that He always loves us enough to continually want to reveal more of Himself to us and through us. We often continue to be anxious about the future, however, and need to remind ourselves of the truth that *God is in control*. We sometimes need to retell the stories of God's constant love and goodness to us by looking back over the years and remembering His protection and hand on our lives. Then we can continue to declare His marvellous deeds today and be confident that He will continue to have His hand on our lives in the future too.

Praise You, God, for all the wonderful things that You have done in my life so far. Please help me to continue to trust in Your future plans for me. Amen.

The second quarter we lived in was a nightmare. The doors wouldn't lock, the oven and the heating didn't work, and a fox had left the remains of several small animals on the patio. My heart cried out, 'Lord, why?!' I felt hard done by. God saw things differently, and began to change my perspective. The church we settled at was located in a poor area of town. One day a girl pointed out a house. 'We used to live there,' she said, 'until my brother's mate put a petrol bomb through our door.' My house worries were nothing in comparison. Suddenly, my house felt safe, I realised it was in a good neighbourhood and my husband had a good job. I started to see that so many people don't have any of those things. It challenged me that I could be doing more for others who had much bigger problems than I did.

In Psalm 72 we see the king pouring

Serve to lead

'For he will deliver the needy who cry out, the afflicted who have no-one to help.' (Psa. 72:12)

out his requests to God; 'help me to be a good and godly ruler, provide everything I need so that I may be a blessing to Your people and meet their needs' (my paraphrase). This prayer is mirrored in Isaiah 61:1, which talks about God's Spirit anointing us to meet the needs of others. Sometimes it can be easy to forget the needs there are around us. Our own problems can seem overwhelming – mine certainly did – but actually reaching out a hand to others who are *more* in need can help us to put our situation into perspective.

Lord, let us help those who are in need and in doing so, be more appreciative of what we ourselves have. Amen.

DAY 78

PSALM 73;
ROMANS 8:28

Yesterday we talked about how God can change the way we see things. I have found that He also has a plan for my life that is far more wonderful than anything I could imagine for myself. My husband and I love Devon and had thought that, once I left the Army, we would find a property on the edge of Dartmoor and retire there with our horses and cats. We looked at other folk who had done it and felt certain that we would be happiest if we did likewise.

However, God had a better idea! On the first day of my resettlement, having ignored the AFCU mailing for a couple of weeks, I sat down for a quiet time and realised that I needed the next edition of my Bible study notes, which would be in the AFCU mailing upstairs. The first thing to fall out was not the Bible study notes, but an advertisement for

He knows best!

'... you hold me by my right hand. You guide me with your counsel, and afterwards you will take me into glory.' (Psa. 73:23–24)

the Executive Officer's job at AFCU HQ in Aldershot, only four miles from home. I was reasonably sure that my heavenly Appointer had my name on that particular posting and, once I was offered the job, knew that yet again God had held me by my right hand and guided me with His counsel. Taking over the job felt like putting on a comfortable pair of old slippers! Truly, '... God works for the good of those who love him, who have been called according to his purpose' (Rom. 8:28).

Lord, help me to trust You that You are working Your purposes out in my life and that everything that happens will ultimately work together for my good. Amen.

DAY 79

PSALM 74;
GALATIANS 5:25

Stop, look and listen!

'It was you who set all the boundaries of the earth; you made both summer and winter.'
(Psa. 74:17)

DAY 80

PSALM 75;
ROMANS 13:1–7

Whilst training at Sandhurst, after yet again not much sleep, we went 'on patrol'. We encountered a training scenario of injured personnel in a minefield. One was writhing around pretending to be in pain in a very realistic manner so I fell to the ground and tried to speak encouragingly to him to calm him down. In a moment of madness, I came up with the bright idea of throwing him a first aid kit. As it was in mid-air, my mistake dawned on me. The Sandhurst instructor looked on in disbelief as of course, if this had been real, the kit would have fallen to the ground and the injured man and I would be no more ...

In today's psalm Mount Zion has been devastated by war. In fact, the ruins described could scarcely be worse if they had been blown to bits by an IED. Everyday life often feels like a minefield

of potential mistakes. I frequently rush headlong into a situation and try to fix things, and then have to extract myself from the muddle, or worse. Why do I do this? Verse 17 reminds us that God is all-powerful, that He knows our boundaries because He created them. If we'd only pause a moment to listen for His 'still, small voice', to ask the Holy Spirit to guide us, then we would allow God into the situation and give Him space to act. Let's pray today for this ability to 'keep in step with the Spirit' (Gal. 5:25).

Father God, help me to pause and listen to You so that I might hear Your still, small voice and know Your will for my life. Amen.

Last week tension enveloped the patch in the lead-up to the publication of a promotion list. There was a mixture of nervous anticipation and dread; who would be cracking open bottles of champagne and who, while outwardly congratulating their peers, would inwardly be wondering why they hadn't made the grade? It is so easy to see things from a purely human point of view. However, today's readings remind us that it is God who promotes.

God has the casting vote, and God determines who is in charge. I find the context surrounding Paul's letter to the Romans helpful when I think of the corrupt tyrants who hold power in some nations today or the incompetent military leaders who have been promoted whilst other more seemingly 'worthy' individuals have been side-lined. When Paul wrote these words, he was not enjoying honourable godly

Promotion prospects

'For promotion cometh neither from the east, nor from the west, nor from the south. But God is the judge: he putteth down one, and setteth up another.' (Psa. 75:6–7, AV)

leadership, but the sort of Caesars who threw Christians to the lions!

We see that God sometimes allows unjust leaders power for the ultimate greater good. Conversely it must therefore be true that some deserving leaders are denied promotion, also for the greater good. This is a hard concept to accept; it means that when we are promoted at work, it is God and not just our own effort behind our success, and that deals a blow to our pride! It also means, when we are not promoted as we deserve, that there is comfort; God has something better; this applies both to us personally and in the wider context.

Lord, help me to see Your perspective and understand more about Your ways. When I don't understand them, help me still to trust that You are God and Your ways are good. Amen.

DAY 81

PSALM 76;
JAMES 4:8

The dogs had haggis for breakfast again. I don't know what tomorrow's offering will be, as it is still defrosting, and has yet to change from a greyish lump into something that might resemble food. It is the same every time we move – emptying the freezer, and digging up the garden to rescue as many of my precious plants as I can physically manage, before the removal lorry arrives. It can be difficult living this sort of nomadic lifestyle but it is probably nothing to what the Jewish people must have felt during some of the turbulent times in their history. I find it hard to imagine what it would have been like to love and serve a powerful, omnipotent, almighty God without knowing the presence of Jesus.

Psalm 76 paints a fearsome picture of God; at His rebuke, whole armies lie dead (v.6). God seems as unrecognisable as the

Uprooting

'From heaven you pronounced judgment, and the land feared and was quiet ...'
(Psa. 76:8)

meat in my freezer! The Old Testament is full of wars and exiles, of beginnings and endings, of the quest for a permanent home. While I can relate to that last point, I usually need to see the events and God Himself through the revelation of the New Testament, otherwise my understanding of who God is becomes as unrooted as the plants in my garden. James instructs us to 'Draw near to God, and He will draw near to you' (NASB) and I want to encourage you to 'wrap your roots around Jesus' as you think about who God is today and consider how you will live for Him in uncertain and changing times.

Lord, You created this world and You rule over everything. Please help me to trust You even when I don't fully understand. Amen.

DAY 82

PSALM 77;
ISAIAH 46:9

Growing up, I was the only Christian in my home, which meant that I lived for the annual Church Youth Group house party. These were amazing times of worshipping with other Christians, learning about God and growing loads in faith. But all too often, this was followed by the crash back to reality upon my return home. The following weeks were always ones of real struggle and darkness, trying to follow Christ on my own. I longed to live and experience life as if I were at a permanent Christian event, rejoicing with God's people.

Thankfully my teenage years are far behind me now and I no longer experience the great highs and lows of emotion in quite the same way! However, over the years there have continued to be times when God has felt very close but also when His presence has felt distant

Remember the good times?

'I thought about the former days, the years of long ago; I remembered my songs in the night.' (Psa. 77:5–6)

or indeed completely absent. Sometimes being with God is the last thing we want to do and we struggle even to pray. We might also wonder, as the psalmist did, whether God has forgotten us. But, wherever we feel we are, God is right there with us, *whether we feel His presence or not*. It can be helpful during such times to look back and remember the occasions when we saw God at work in our lives. As you go through today take time to recall times of God's blessings and give Him thanks.

Lord, when You feel far away and distant, help me to remember and praise You for all the ways that You have blessed me in the past, that I might once again sing Your songs of joy. Amen.

DAY 83

PSALM 78:1–39;
2 CHRONICLES 7:14

Before joining the Army, I was a teacher in Birmingham and I remember going to a musical in the city centre called *If My People*. Written by Jimmy and Carole Owens and narrated by Pat Boone, it was a call to the Church in Britain, based on 2 Chronicles 7:14, to start praying for a return to Christian values and seek God for a revival in our country. That inspiring message was in 1975. How much more does the Church need this message today! It is so easy to be diverted from working and praying towards this vision.

The psalmist reminds us how the Israelites, despite the signs and wonders that God had performed in bringing them out of Egypt and into the promised land, turned their backs on God, forgot what He had done for them and refused to live by His law. Yet, however much they turned from Him, when they sought Him, He

Law-breakers

'... they did not keep God's covenant and refused to live by his law. They forgot what he had done, the wonders he had shown them.' (Psa. 78:10–11)

DAY 84

PSALM 78:40–72;
JOHN 20:29

Believing the impossible

'They did not remember his power ... the day he displayed his miraculous signs in Egypt, his wonders in the region of Zoan.' (Psa. 78:42–43)

would be merciful, forgive their sins and not destroy them (vv.38–39).

As a nation and as individuals, we need to turn back to God and pray for mercy and forgiveness before we experience His judgment. Never has our nation been in greater need of intercessors to 'humble [themselves] and pray and seek his face' on behalf of our country. Will you cry out to God for forgiveness for our corporate sin? Perhaps, more practically, we could all consider getting together with other Christians to conduct prayer walks around our places of work and leisure? You might even write to your MP!

Lord, as a nation we have turned from You and broken Your laws. Forgive us, I pray, and heal our land. Amen.

I was brought up to believe in God, but also to have a logical mind. Although my faith in God has increased over the years, the underlying belief in science and evidence has remained. After having our first child I was told that I had had a premature menopause and would not be able to have another child. My husband and I were very disappointed, as especially with moving frequently we wanted our child to have a sibling to help with the instability. We reluctantly learned to cope with the fact that this would never be possible.

Some years later, after an incredible time of prayer, I discovered that I was pregnant! The medical professionals were as surprised as we were and it has been great to tell people of this miracle! More significantly, it has challenged my view of God and broadened my belief in

His power. Reading the Old Testament I now see countless examples of where God chooses to use miracles of nature to bless His people, whether this is through pregnancy in old age, plagues against their enemies or help in crossing the Red Sea. I'm so grateful for this second child and realise that I had taken my first baby for granted. God has opened my eyes and shown me that He is truly the God of the impossible. Have you limited God's power in your own mind? Why not ask Him to increase your vision?

Lord, thank You for Your hold on my life. I'm sorry for the times when I have taken things for granted; help me to notice the blessings that You give me and to trust in You more fully. Amen.

DAY 85

PSALM 79;
JAMES 4:2

Lord, hear my prayer!

'God! Barbarians have broken into your home, violated your holy temple, left Jerusalem a pile of rubble!'
(**Psa. 79:1,** *The Message*)

I used to dream of the days when we could move out of our married quarter and into our own home. Then we could paint the walls some colour other than magnolia and strip the carpet off the floor. Finally, that glorious day came, we moved into our own house and … the shower broke, the aerial failed to receive a television picture, the fireplace smoked and the washing machine discharged all its water under the lino on the kitchen floor! How I longed to pick up the phone to the Defence Housing Agency and wail, 'This is your mess, come and sort it out!'

There is a similar heart's cry by the psalmist to God in today's psalm. You can hear him thinking, 'God, where are You? Look what is happening here on Your own patch! Come and put it right.' Too often I know I try and muddle through the mess in my own life, when God is just waiting

to hear me call. I can be as honest and real about the chaos as I like with Him, and He can always fix it. What is more, He has already paid the price in full and he doesn't have a call-out fee! That is great news because it means I don't have to wait for an emergency. Unlike the MoD contract plumber, it is just as important to Him to fix a little dripping tap as it is to repair a major leak.

Reflect today on the state of your 'spiritual house'. What major or minor repairs need attending to? Call on God and ask Him to put things right.

DAY 86

PSALM 80;
NUMBERS 6:24–26

Many of the Psalms are cries of misery to God. Psalm 80 is full of 'How long?' and 'Why?' As an Army wife, when I'm left alone for six months or more to cope with all that life throws at me, I often feel like crying out, 'How much longer?' or, 'You've only just come back, why do you have to go again?' Often I'm left to answer our children who don't understand why Daddy has gone away – again! Sound familiar?

Sometimes, I've followed my husband on postings to places I don't want to go, and where there's no one I know. In some places it's been very hard to make friends. The time I have to spend there is a drudgery, day after day. Like the Israelites, I feel as though I am in exile and I cry out, 'How much longer will I have to suffer this?'

I have discovered that help is at hand! If I cry to God and ask that He 'shines His

Let the Son shine

'Restore us, O God; make your face shine upon us, that we may be saved.'
(Psa. 80:3)

face' on me, my view of where I am can be completely changed. It could still be a difficult posting, but if I look to and for God every day, my misery will slowly be lifted as He gives me a fresh perspective and new insights into my time 'in exile'.

Lord God, You know that in some areas my life is difficult and I sometimes feel that You have left. Help me never to give up. Lord, I am crying out to You today; please show me Your face and restore my hope and peace. Amen.

DAY 87

PSALM 81;
JOHN 6:25–59

It is said that an army marches on its stomach. The Military takes food very seriously – so much so that it is even a chargeable offence to miss breakfast! Why? Because a soldier's job can be hard work at times. He (or she) needs the proper nourishment to enable him to do his job properly. If he is weak through lack of food, he will be a liability to himself and his team. On operations, this could mean the difference between life and death.

Just as we need food to nourish our physical bodies, so we also need *spiritual* food to nourish our relationship with Jesus. Luckily, we don't need to count calories on our spiritual diet! In fact, daily over-indulging is recommended! Over-indulging on the Word is a sure-fire way to keep us spiritually strong and healthy. It nourishes our bodies so that we can live a victorious life. It feeds us the

Spiritual scoff!

'I am the LORD your God … Open wide your mouth and I will fill it.' (Psa. 81:10)

fruit of the Spirit, which gives us strength for whatever life throws at us. It gives us wisdom to help our family and friends. Jesus said that He is the 'bread of life' and if we come to Him, we will never go hungry or thirsty. Are you hungry and thirsty? Don't skip your spiritual breakfast and risk getting charged on the day of judgment.

The food we work for eventually spoils, but Jesus offers a food that endures for eternity. He says, 'If my people would but listen to me ... you would be fed with the finest of wheat; with honey from the rock I would satisfy you' (Psa. 81:13–16).

Father, thank You for sending Jesus to be living bread for us. Help us to be proactive about our spiritual diet as much as our physical food. Amen.

DAY 88

PSALM 82;
MATTHEW 9:35–38

Can I help you?

'Ignorant judges! Head-in-the-sand judges!
They haven't a clue to what's going on.
And … the world's coming unglued.'
(Psa. 82:5, *The Message*)

This is a very hard psalm to make sense of, but if you can read it in *The Message* version it is well worth it! Basically, God is judging those He has put in positions of authority and they aren't coming out of it very well! But the lesson here isn't just for judges. We all have a responsibility to look out for other people – especially those who are vulnerable. It is unlikely that any of us will have to face someone who has committed murder, let alone judge them, but what about the other types of people that get a mention in this passage: 'defend the defenceless, make sure that underdogs get a fair break … stand up for the powerless …' (vv.2–4)?

To be honest it all sounds very worthy, even out of my league, but God keeps bringing people and situations to mind where I can be His hands and feet: the new colleague who is finding it hard to cope; the young mum who is struggling while her husband is away; the child who is being bullied at the bus stop outside our house. Then there are those who don't quite 'fit' into the military mould, people who would value a kind word or a helping hand. Sometimes it doesn't even take a lot of effort on my part but for those on the receiving end, it could make all the difference. Let's be more aware of people around us and, like Jesus, have compassion for their needs.

Dear Lord, open my eyes to see people through Your eyes. Show me how people around me are feeling and give me the courage to make a difference in their lives. Amen.

DAY 89

PSALM 83;
GALATIANS 5:13–15

Whilst on operations in Bosnia we faced the threat of incoming fire; both from mortars aimed at our camp, and from celebratory gunfire from one faction or another. The latter meant a trail of munitions dropping to the ground under gravity, which could be as dangerous as direct targeting. However, the most serious injury during our tour was from a fire one night in the sleeping accommodation. The lightweight portacabins were tightly packed into a small area and the blaze quickly engulfed one, melting it and spreading to neighbouring rooms. Fortunately, someone spotted it quickly and we were able to evacuate and dowse the area sufficiently to prevent the whole camp being destroyed. The cause of the fire was not fully ascertained, but was either poor electrical work or the electrician falling asleep while smoking. Either way, it was not deliberate,

Friendly fire?

'As fire consumes the forest or a flame sets the mountain ablaze …' (Psa. 83:14)

but down to negligence or disobedience. Somehow, it seems far more wasteful and pointless when the injury or damage is avoidable, rather than caused by a deliberate act of aggression or opposition.

Disobedience to God, or incompetence in following His ways, can also be more disastrous to the Church than the best efforts of any atheist group. Through daily repentance, earnestly seeking to become more like Christ and by being accountable to other Christians, we can avoid friendly-fire incidents and contribute to the building up, rather than the breaking down, of God's kingdom.

Lord, forgive me when I am negligent or disobedient. Help me to grow more like Your Son, Jesus, and to love my neighbour as myself. Amen.

DAY 90

PSALM 84;
ACTS 2:42–47

Whilst living in Brunei, a Muslim state where Christians do not enjoy the same freedom to worship as they do in the UK, the Lord brought me into contact with a very diverse group of Christian women, all of different nationalities. We enjoyed wonderful fellowship together in one another's homes and were very aware of God's presence with us as we met. We gained much spiritual refreshment in an otherwise very 'dry land'. Having to say goodbye to these dear friends and leave behind my church family and all that I had come to enjoy being a part of was not easy – it never is.

Sometimes I experience a great sense of loss, an overwhelming sense of detachment, when arriving at a new location. Whilst going through this unsettled period, I have come to realise that my deepest yearning is for the

Coming home

'One day spent in your house, this beautiful place of worship, beats thousands spent on Greek island beaches.' (Psa. 84:10, *The Message*)

fellowship and bond I have had with my Christian family. I have learnt that seeking a place where God is worshipped, where the people love Him and honour His Word, has to be a priority when moving into a new area. I pray that I will be guided to such a place. When I am in that place, even if it's initially on the periphery, I know at once that I belong. I feel secure, protected and reassured that I am a member of God's family. *It's like coming home.* On reflection, I see how God's provision has been perfect for each location.

Dear Lord, thank You that we can worship in freedom, for the fellowship of my church family and for the sanctuary of Your 'dwelling-place'. Amen.

DAY 91

PSALM 85;
ACTS 3:19

Ready for 'stand to'?

'Surely his salvation is near to those who fear him, so our land will be filled with his glory.' (Psa. 85:9, NLT)

DAY 92

PSALM 86;
MATTHEW 13:5

My heart lurches every time I hear of the death of a serving military person – this week it was an RAF pilot; one of those out 'of the blue' incidents that ring all the alarm bells in a military wife's mind. After the initial shock, questioning who and what was involved, come the 'How did this happen?' and 'What could have been done to avoid it?' questions, and then further on I start to wonder. 'Did they know God?' 'Were they saved?'

We never know when our last day will be. However, we have the confidence that we worship a God who is always listening out for us and whose watchful eye is always upon us. We only need to turn to Him and He will be found. He is always waiting with outstretched arms and a love fit to burst. But we do need to turn to Him and repent of all that we have done wrong, and accept His love in order to 'know' that

we are His own and to have the certainty that one day we will spend eternity with Him. We have a responsibility to pray for others that they too may come to know the all-encompassing and glorious love of our precious Saviour. As we see other people come to faith in Christ, so we will see His glory beginning to impact in our own families and communities.

Lord, thank You that You are always near to each one of us. I pray today for those known to us who do not know Your saving love. Please speak to their hearts through the power of Your Holy Spirit. Amen.

My sister once told me that I am a bit of a social chameleon: I have an ability to read the environment and change to fit in with it! This has been a useful tool in the Military where I am required to have a 'flexible approach', an ability to 'get along' with folk, and say the right things to the right people. I am expected to conform to expectation and to influence others. I am encouraged to melt into my environment, to use camouflage to conceal my true identity.

However, after contemplating my sister's comment, I realised God doesn't want me to be like that at all! This is because what happens is that I fail to share who I really am with God. My heart becomes divided in its loyalties. I wonder, 'Are my words bringing God's love and truth to people, or am I merely oiling the wheels of promotion or smoothing

An undivided heart

'... give me an undivided heart, that I may fear your name.' (Psa. 86:11)

working relationships for my own gain?' I know there are gaps in my character where I have failed to accept God's total sovereignty. This shallow, rootless faith (Matt. 13:5) is a pale reflection of what life in Christ is designed to be. God wants us to accept Him into every thought, feeling, and moment, so that we can reach our full potential in Him.

What parts of who you are and how you relate to your environment might you have forgotten to give over to God? Which particular bit could you talk to Him about today?

DAY 93

PSALM 87;
ROMANS 12:1–2

Before I joined the Army, I used to attend a church in Birmingham where I was a member of the worship dance group. Through dance we sought to interpret the words of various worship songs. We met together weekly for prayer and rehearsal and from time to time danced in church services and went on tour to a number of Scandinavian countries. One of the songs we used to dance to was based on Psalm 87:3–5, and I cannot now read this psalm without remembering the joy of dancing in worship to God. In Romans, Paul urges us to offer our bodies as living sacrifices, which is our spiritual act of worship (Rom. 12:1) and I found that through physical movement, I was able to worship God in a way at least as meaningful as through singing (which I'm not very good at!).

I had little or no opportunity to

Lord of the dance

'Glorious things are said of you [Zion], O city of God ...' (Psa. 87:3)

worship God through dance in corporate acts of worship during my Army career, and whilst I would occasionally dance in private during my own Quiet Times, it was something that I missed. When the opportunity presented itself, I was very happy to offer to run a worship dance session at a recent AFCU Ladies' weekend. I was thrilled that several women bore testimony to finding a new freedom to worship through movement. King David danced before the Lord with all his might (2 Sam. 6:14). How do you worship God with all *your* might? Is dance something that you might consider?

Lord, help me to worship You with all of my being and to be open to new ways of expressing my love for You. Amen.

DAY 94

My husband has the habit of coming into our bedroom and turning the light on immediately, even if he knows that I am already in bed trying to get to sleep. I can hide under the bedclothes to block out the light but it is still there! It is physically impossible to have both light *and* darkness at the same time. The Bible says that Jesus came into the world to dispel the darkness and 'in [God] there is no darkness at all' (1 John 1:5).

I am not saying here that for the Christian there are no dark places, because that is clearly not the case for many of us. In today's reading the psalmist describes feeling as if he were 'in the lowest pit, the darkest depths' (v.6). He feels abandoned by God, is clearly depressed, and probably oppressed too. We can all get trapped in a web of lies spun by the devil, the father of lies, and this can

Dispelling the darkness

'Are your wonders known in the place of darkness, or your righteous deeds in the land of oblivion?' (Psa. 88:12)

make life hard. Have you ever heard Satan whisper, 'You are not worthy', or 'You are unlovable', or 'It's your fault', or 'You get in the way'? Let God's truth shine light in these dark places, expose the lies, and cut you free from them. Hold on to the fact that you are loved by God (John 3:16), and Jesus came into the world to be the Light and to dispel all the darkness.

Lord, please help me to listen to Your truth revealed to us in Your Word and not to be taken in by the devil's lies, no matter how I feel. Amen.

DAY 95

I have a question, 'Why do I find it easier to see God in His role of judge, condemning me for my sin, than to see His unfailing love and truth towards me?' Psalm 89 tells us that His throne is founded on 'righteousness and justice' but when times are difficult I still cry out in anger and frustration, 'Why me Lord?', 'Life seems so unfair!' It can feel like I am being punished.

I have been challenged recently to start looking more positively at both my life and the view that God has of me, although my personal history means that I am prone to take a negative view of life. Constant moving with the Military has aggravated the sense I have of injustice: 'Why did I have to marry a pilot? Why can't we have a "normal life"?' Lately though, I have found an increasing comfort in knowing that God *sees* these

Strong foundations

'Righteousness and justice are the foundation of your throne; love and faithfulness go before you.' (Psa. 89:14)

DAY 96

PSALM 89:19–52;
ISAIAH 32:2

Rock-like strength

'He will call out to me, "You are my Father, my God, the Rock my Saviour."' (Psa. 89:26)

struggles. In Isaiah 61, God says that He 'will faithfully reward [His] people for their suffering' (v.8, NLT). Those rewards don't necessarily always come where or when we feel we need them. However, if God has 'unfailing love and truth' walking as His 'attendants' and His pillars are 'righteousness and justice' then it is not possible for Him to let any one of us down. He has to be true to His unfailing love for us. Be warned though, His plan is usually much more long term than we would like, and things often come about in ways we don't expect!

Lord, help me to trust in You. Keep my eyes focused on You, looking forward to the delights You have for me. Amen.

A few weeks ago during the stress of another move, my seven-year-old asked me 'If you and Daddy ever split up what will happen to me?' He had misunderstood a conversation between the two of us and thought that we were breaking up. Thinking about it a little more, I began to see that what he wanted was the assurance that Mummy and Daddy would be there no matter what, particularly during times of great change and upheaval in his life. Children need rock-like stability to feel safe. I wanted to promise him that we would always be there but had a dawning realisation that this is not a promise I *could* make and keep. We simply don't know what the future holds; one day we will all die, and we don't even know when that day will be.

But, the Bible tells me that God is a rock. A rock symbolises strength, security and permanence. In Christ, we too can reflect this rock-like image to our families and other people close to us. While in all honesty I can not promise my son I will be there forever, I can give him my best every day while I am here and through that, guide him to the true Rock, Jesus. So for now I stand here with him in the cool shadow from the big Rock in what can feel like a hot, weary place and, as he grows up I pray he will look and see the much bigger shadow surrounding mine, which is God over us both.

Lord, help me to stand firm on You, my Rock that I may show Your likeness to others through me. Amen.

DAY 97

Countdown!

'Teach us to number our days aright that we may gain a heart of wisdom.' (Psa. 90:12)

I loved it when my children first learned to speak and then to count. But soon they realised they could count days and now we get 'Only 364 days left till my birthday' and 'Only six months left until Christmas'! Sometimes it's good to count. We make a chuff chart to mark off the days until Daddy comes home; I count days to the next move because I love going to new places.

You know the saying 'A watched pot never boils'? The same is true about time. The few days on R&R go quicker than a weekend spent alone. When my husband is away, it is only natural to want him back home and I look forward to that day, but I have to be careful not to miss out on things that are going on each day. So what is the solution?

This psalm encourages us to find God's meaning and purpose in the days we have. I sometimes complete an online course or get a group of friends to teach me something new, or I attend one of the trips that the Wives' Club organises to help pass the time, but even more than that I want to ask God to give me His perspective on the days I have on earth and how to fill them. I don't just want to spend life counting days – I want God to help me make the days count!

Lord, please be with me through the long days when life seems too hard to handle. Give me strength to face each day with hope and joy – so that each one counts. Amen.

DAY 98

Fear (False Evidence Appearing Real) can often surface, especially at night, and particularly when my husband is deployed. I remember how the Lord clearly gave me the scripture from this psalm, especially verses 5 and 6 whilst we were on exchange in Darwin, Australia. My husband was away at sea and one of my biggest fears came at night in the form of cockroaches that 'stalked in the darkness'. One night I remember a huge cockroach running along the landing and disappearing into my new-born son's room. I had to decide whether to just ignore it or use the toxic roach spray – I am afraid the roach spray won!

Psalm 91 is commonly known as the 'Psalm of Protection'. It is famous for comparing the love and protection of the Lord to several beautiful images. God is a 'shelter' and we live in His 'shadow'.

DAY 99

Fear nought

'You will not fear the terror of night ... nor the pestilence that stalks in the darkness ...' (Psa. 91:5–6)

The Lord is a 'refuge' and a 'fortress' and God covers us with His feathers and wings. It is a psalm used in times of danger and exposure, or for challenging the power of evil. I gained such a peace about 'the creatures of the night' after finding this scripture. It was a reminder to me that God cares about every little detail of our lives, especially the things that worry us.

Staying out of fear mode is essential for the victorious living that God intends us to enjoy. This victorious living requires a proactive response to adversity.

Dear Lord, thank You that You constantly watch over us. Help us to hand all of our fears over to You, especially when we feel overwhelmed by them. Amen.

Growing tall and hardy

'The righteous will flourish like a palm tree, they will grow like a cedar of Lebanon ...' (Psa. 92:12)

Upon returning to the Mess after a long weekend I was horrified to find that my newly acquired plant, purchased to breathe life into my gaunt and featureless cabin, had wilted. I checked the label: 'Easter Cactus'. I begged to differ. It had looked the hardy type, but I was disappointed at its lack of resilience; it just couldn't hack the austere microclimate that I tend to create for my plants!

This psalm contrasts those without the Lord – the grass that effortlessly springs up and is easily destroyed, to the righteous, – the strong and mighty palms and cedars of Lebanon. Whilst grass withers and blows away, palms and cedars grow very tall, slowly, heavenwards, and are not affected by long bouts of bad weather. They survive drought (palms in the desert) and frost (cedar in the mountains), their hardy leaves remain verdant, no matter what the season.

As we begin to live in God, we too will begin to become like a palm or a cedar; perennial and resilient. Cedar wood was used to build the Jewish Temple because it lasted well. Palm trees have traditionally been planted within the perimeters of holy places and flourish for generations. They produce fruit into old age, in the same way that mature Christians produce good spiritual fruit. In growing in Him, God grants us strength to survive, but more than that, to flourish, and for that to last for generations.

God promises to grow us. If we are pursuing Him we will not be left to become stagnant. He urges us to crave pure spiritual milk so that we may grow up into everlasting life.

DAY 100

PSALM 93;
MATTHEW 24

Beyond all doubt

**'The Lord reigns, he is robed in majesty
... and is armed with strength. The world
is firmly established; it cannot be moved.'**
(Psa. 93:1)

Every few years someone makes a prediction that the world is going to end. These stories are often given quite a lot of media coverage. Inevitably, vulnerable people have fallen prey to these false prophecies. Sometimes they have been so convinced the world will end that they have taken drastic action and sold houses or had pets put down.* I have often come across a cynicism within the Military to disbelieve anything that cannot be scientifically weighed and measured, and against the backdrop of this magnificent psalm these predictions seem about as plausible as the children's fairy tale about Chicken-Licken, who thought the sky was falling down when an acorn once dropped on her head!

Of course as a Christian, I do believe that one day, when Jesus returns to judge the earth, there will be a brand-new heaven and a new earth, even more wonderful

and magnificent than this one. This isn't some 'pie in the sky' prophecy made by a madman but a genuine prophetic revelation given by Jesus. One day this world *will* end, but rather than dread it we can eagerly anticipate it, because when it happens Jesus will also return to reign on earth as King.

Equally, we need not fear when we hear a 'prophecy' concerning a specific date, not because we are cynical, but because Jesus tells us that only God the Father knows those details. Instead, we can praise God for this earth as a small symbol of His strength and majesty which one day will be eclipsed completely by the sheer breadth and wonder of His eternal kingdom.

Lord, thank You for Your awesome might and power. Thank You that we have the secure hope of Jesus' return and a new heaven and earth established by You. Amen.

*Responses to Harold Camping's prediction, 21 May 2011.

DAY 101

PSALM 94;
JOHN 15:9–17

I was working in a busy, overstretched garrison health centre supporting a deployed brigade and its temporarily abandoned families. My patient had just left and I realised that I had forgotten to check his blood pressure. I began to feel hot and sweaty, and my heart was racing. I tried to decide what to do about the missed blood pressure, but all I wanted was to go and hide somewhere. Perhaps I was coming down with swine flu? The sensations in my body got worse, and the seemingly simple decision got harder to make. I realised that I was experiencing my first panic attack. This heralded the beginning of a period of being unwell; my body was telling me that there was something really 'not right' in my soul and my spirit. The next twelve months became a tangle of time off work ill, explaining myself to the Commanding Officer, appointments, medication,

Provision in despair

'When I said, "My foot is slipping,"
your love, O LORD, supported me.'
(Psa. 94:18)

counselling, and tears – many, many tears. My foot had slipped in a big way, and I had fallen on my knees.

The Lord provided for me in ways I couldn't think to ask: fantastic understanding and support from my military boss; deepening of relationships in my church; a chance to move out of the wire; prayer, prayer, and more prayer support; the list goes on. The personal growth that I experienced was deeply painful to acquire, but essential to becoming more enmeshed in God. Is your 'foot slipping' today? God desires to support you just as much as He has supported me. All we need to do is 'remain in Him'.

Lord, when anxiety is great within me, may Your consolation bring joy to my soul. Amen.

DAY 102

PSALM 95;
1 CHRONICLES 16:23–36

My favourite country is Switzerland, where God's creation is so beautiful; the mountains and chalets with the wild flowers in summer and the snow in the winter. The atmosphere always seems special, and I love going there at any time of year; my heart is full of grateful praise. For military families, frequent postings give us the opportunity to seek out the beauty of another area. It could be a National Trust property or RHS garden. Holidays are also often a time to see a sunset over a beach or be amazed at God's beauty in another country. We see the Lord's hand in the flowers around us, the children playing happily, a new baby, good health or our home. Let's raise our hearts to Him in songs of praise and thanksgiving for all the blessings that He has lavished on us.

Psalm 95 is also called the Venite (from

Amazing beauty

'Come, let us bow down in worship, let us kneel before the LORD our Maker ...'
(Psa. 95:6)

the Latin, 'O come'). God is our strength who delivers us so we can respond with thanksgiving. The Lord loves to hear the praises of His people. How often do I sing out His praises from a heart filled with joy and thankfulness? Probably not as often as I should! Both the psalmist and chronicler declare He is the Creator God, yet He cares for each of us and our response is to kneel in awe. Do we take time to praise and worship Him in the way He deserves?

Lord, I lift my heart in thankful praise for all the blessings You bestow upon me. You show Your grace in giving me many things I don't deserve; You prove Your mercy when You don't give me what I do deserve. Amen.

DAY 103

Sound the fanfare!

'Declare his glory among the nations, his marvellous deeds among all peoples.'
(Psa. 96:3)

We had moved into another quarter, but this move was different. My husband had been promoted and was now an officer so we now lived on the officers' patch. It's hard to explain my overwhelming feelings of inadequacy. I left school with only a few qualifications and suddenly here I was, living amongst teachers and well-educated people. How could I possibly make friends with them?

Soon after moving in I went on an AFCU Ladies' weekend, where I took the opportunity to pour out my feelings to God. I explained that I was certain the move was wrong and surely He couldn't expect me to share His message of hope with such well-balanced and educated people. That same evening, I picked up the book *Don't Just Stand There, Pray Something!* and continued to read from page 75 where I had left a bookmarker

some time before. I read, 'Do you think you just lucked into that particular house on that particular street? Could it be that God wanted a harvest there and you are the seed He planted?'*

What a privilege it is to move among nations but also to cross all boundaries. With God we can reach out to those around us. After all, we are chosen and dearly loved children of the living God, no matter how inadequate we may feel and He has promised to be with us always. Our God is *great* so let us declare it among all peoples!

Almighty Father, forgive me for doubting all that You can do in and through me. Please help me to be more open to Your leading and enabling. Amen.

---

*Ronald Dunn, *Don't Just Stand There, Pray Something: Discover the Incredible Power of Intercessory Prayer* (Marshall Pickering, new edition, 2001), p.75.

DAY 104

Some time ago I was talking with an airman who had one last chance to pass his fitness test before he faced an administrative discharge. He was being mocked by his colleagues. Feeling bold, I prayed for him in front of them before he went to take his test. Guess what? He passed!

On another occasion I was talking with a serving policeman who had just received a posting that meant weekend-commuting home to see his family. He was really upset about this and I said I would pray for him too. Weeks later, my prayer was answered and his posting was changed to one a few miles away from the family home instead. Quite a miracle in the Military! He asked me why God would be interested in him when there was so much going on around the world. The answer? God is mighty and powerful – truly the 'mountains melt like

Who cares? He cares!

'The mountains melt like wax before the LORD …' (Psa. 97:5)

wax' before Him – but He also cares for the needs of the individual, whether they are big or small.

The amazing thing about God is that He, who created the universe, is the same God who came to earth to die on a cross for our sins. If you ever doubt God's love and concern for you, think about Jesus Christ and what He's done for you. He created you and cares about you so deeply that He died for you. He *loves* you. So stop doubting.

Lord, there are things in my life that make me feel You're distant and that You don't care for me. Help me to look to Jesus to see how much You really do love me. Amen.

DAY 105

PSALM 98;
EPHESIANS 5:19–20

Having been with the Armed Forces all my life I can truly say I am used to the word 'new'. New quarter, new job, new friends, new school, new church … the list goes on. I believed I was quite a dab hand at new things until I attended a church in Scotland. Their worship style was completely out of my comfort zone, not only did they raise their hands but they also danced and sang in tongues. This left me feeling like a goldfish on the outside of the bowl! It didn't help that I was going through an emotional rollercoaster; how on earth was I going to have fun in worship when my inner being was so down in the dumps?

One week the pastor spoke about sacrifice and sacrificial worship. He explained that to worship when we did not feel able to was actually a sacrificial gift and was a wonderful thing to give

A new song

'Sing to the LORD a new song, for he has done marvellous things; his right hand and his holy arm have worked salvation for him.' (Psa. 98:1)

our Lord who has sacrificially given everything for us. He acknowledged that it was a difficult step but it was up to us to take that step; no one could do it for us. I cried out to God as I felt that I was such a failure for not being able to praise Him as I should. I took a small step towards trusting His enabling. Suddenly, I found myself swimming with them all; what fun we had lifting up the name of the Lord!

Heavenly Father, examine my heart, strengthen my weak limbs and fill me with the joy of Your salvation that I may glorify You in Your sanctuary. Amen.

DAY 106

PSALM 99;
EXODUS 14:13–20

The pillar of cloud

'He spoke from the pillar of cloud. And they did what he said; they kept the law he gave them.' (Psa. 99:7, *The Message*)

On my last operational tour, we used to travel everywhere in convoys of two or three vehicles. As well as being heavily armoured the vehicles were fitted with Electronic Counter Measures (ECM) equipment. The ECM emitted a sort of protective bubble, which helped to protect vehicles from Improvised Explosive Devices (IEDs). In an environment where there was a constant threat of an IED or suicide attack, I always felt safer travelling with this extra level of protection. It was my security blanket and it helped me to feel calmer.

I remember having to come back to base one day in a foreign vehicle, which did not have ECM. I recall feeling extremely vulnerable and exposed in the drive across the city. The ECM reminds me of the way that God went ahead of the Israelites in a pillar of cloud, offering them guidance and protection. All they had to do was follow and stay close. Are you frightened? Do you feel threatened? Do you feel vulnerable and exposed? I urge you to put on your protective blanket, Jesus, and wrap Him tightly around you. 2 Peter 1:3 says that 'His divine power has given us everything we need for life ...' When you ask Jesus into your life, you are given *everything* you need to get through your trials. You are protected. Just follow and keep Him close. 'The LORD will fight for you; you need only to be still' (Exod. 14:14).

Lord, thank You that You always protect and watch over me. Help me to put my trust in You and not in man-made security. Amen.

DAY 107

PSALM 100;
1 THESSALONIANS 5:18

Do you ever get that feeling of 'Here I go again'? I have struggled with it a lot lately – when I was alone at home whilst my husband was deployed to Afghanistan. I frequently had that grey feeling as I put away yet another batch of clothes, with the washing machine already on again, cleaning to be done and the endless tidying up of the house. Then, of course, I would need to go to the shops to buy something to make yet another family meal. God tells us to do all tasks with thanks but, on these monotonous days, I found it really hard to give thanks when it seemed to be one endless cycle of jobs.

To help me focus on Jesus I would turn up the volume on the stereo and blast my praise music out so loud that I would end up smiling and giving thanks, singing at the top of my voice and thanking God that I actually *had* a home to clean, children

Raise the roof

'Enter his gates with thanksgiving and his courts with praise; give thanks to him and praise his name.' (Psa. 100:4)

to clear up after and money to put food on the table. I found that through singing simple praise songs and focusing on Jesus, my spirits were lifted and mundane jobs became easier to bear.

Go on … give it a try … no one can see (or hear!) you – except God! Praise Jesus at the top of your voice and feel the joy rise up inside!

Lord, in the dark times when life's jobs get me down, let me turn to You with all that is in my heart and praise You that Your love endures forever. Amen.

DAY 108

PSALM 101;
MATTHEW 28:20

I have the patience of … well, nothing! Every time I ask God for more, I seem to be tested and consequently find myself in a long, frustrating queue. Since joining the Army, to be honest, my patience has been tested most days; either due to the 'hurry up and wait' mentality or just due to unforeseeable delays. An all-time low for me though was the journey back from Iraq which took eighty-four hours, five airports and many queues. The most frustrating part was not knowing just when we would all return to our loved ones. It was the 'nearly but not quite' that was difficult. And each hour spent waiting ate into much needed R&R! At times it was too easy to take out our frustrations on officials or to blame the RAF!

When I first became a Christian, I was mindful of Psalm 101, which reminds us that God's eye is upon us and advises

Hurry up and wait!

'My eyes will be on the faithful in the land, that they may dwell with me; the one whose walk is blameless will minister to me.' (Psa. 101:6, NIV, 2011)

caution in how we speak and act. I prayed each day that God would help me to control my tongue in a bid to stop swearing. This psalm is also a useful prayer to help us to treat all people with patience and respect even when we want to shout at them! In my travels around the world with the Army, my patience continues to be tested, but I now try to remember the words of Jesus that, wherever I am and whatever I am doing, He promises to be ' … with [me] always, to the very end of the age' (Matt. 28:20), even when I am crabby!

Compassionate, gracious, loving Lord, control my tongue and help me to be patient with others today. Amen.

DAY 109

PSALM 102;
JAMES 1:2–3

How are you *really* feeling today? This psalm is entitled, 'A prayer of an afflicted man'. It comes smack bang in the middle of some of the most joyful psalms, and yet the author describes the depth of his sorrow: his insomnia, his loss of appetite and the tears that mingle with his drink. It sounds like he might be suffering from some of the symptoms of depression. These feelings are very common, especially so in women apparently, and can come to a head when they are on their own with small children. I've been there and I wasn't abandoned with lots of children! But certainly the stresses of service life contributed.

During that time, I found it so important to allow God into the very depths of my experience but, in fact, He was already there. It is vital to allow our emotions time to be released, actively sharing them with God; maybe in prayer, in a letter, through tears, or with a friend.

As the Psalms demonstrate, this can be very liberating and healing because God accepts us just as we are. There are no parts of us that are 'off limits' for Him and, as our reading from James shows, He uses these occasions to mature our characters. Many of us may find it hard to allow Him in at these times, putting up a wall of silence. It can be equally hard to admit that we need practical help, whether that is through medication, counselling or allowing a friend to know how low we really feel. But, God is faithful; He *will* respond to the prayer of the destitute.

Abba, Father, help me to be the real me, the whole me – with You. Amen.

Keeping it real

'He will respond to the prayer of the destitute ...' (Psa. 102:17)

DAY 110

PSALM 103;
LUKE 15:1–7

In Kosovo in 1999 we set up camp on the Goles Heights above Pristina airfield. We'd been eating dry rations for the past month; corned-beef hash had lost its appeal! Within hours of the Serbian withdrawal, the Kosovo Albanians began to return from the refugee camps to their burnt-out village homes. Two days later a little line of people began to pick their way up the mountain to our camp, bringing gifts of milk and freshly baked bread. I was overwhelmed and humbled by this outpouring of love and generosity. It was a small reflection of how lavishly God loves us. I love Psalm 103; in times of real hardship God pours out love beyond what we can ask or imagine. He 'satisfies [our] desires with good things' (v.5). I remember the extravagant joy of the refugees as they literally pelted our convoy with plums and cheered as we drove into Kosovo.

DAY 111

PSALM 104:1–18;
MATTHEW 28:18–20

Fresh rations!

'The LORD is compassionate and gracious, slow to anger, abounding in love.' (Psa. 103:8)

Their generosity went beyond mere gratitude. Their actions proved they harboured no resentment. In the same way verse 10 says God 'does not treat us as our sins deserve or repay us according to our iniquities'. I saw that in action when I met a father who had lost his children during the NATO airstrikes. The interpreter explained that the father held no grudge against us. This same type of free forgiveness is the glorious gift that God offers to each one of us like the good shepherd in Luke who went after the one sheep that was lost. Why not ask *Him* for more of His abounding love today?

Father God, I want to praise You with my inmost being for Your extravagant love and complete forgiveness. Amen.

What a way to start …! 'Praise the LORD, O my soul' (v.1), because praising Him with just our lips isn't enough – our *souls* connect with God when we praise Him with our whole being. How do we get that connection? Looking further on into this psalm gives us reasons to go 'Wow!' When we marvel at creation, our souls can be lifted out of the dreariness of everyday life. I'm currently enjoying a rare moment in my garden with a coffee writing this – it's too cold to be out here, but, with a blanket I can enjoy the sunshine and birdsong and find myself more connected.

Staying connected to a community when you're always on the move is hard. I am about to leave a fabulous church and group of friends behind me to move with my husband to his new posting. How will I connect with the next group of mums in the new playground? Over the years, God

Get connected!

'Praise the LORD, O my soul. O LORD my God, you are very great; you are clothed with splendour and majesty.' (Psa. 104:1)

has shown me when I'm frustrated and emotional about moving on, that He will never break His connection with me. In Matthew 28:20 Jesus says to His disciples, '… surely I am with you always, to the very end of the age'. Jesus also promised them a Helper, the Holy Spirit, who made them feel bold when they were scared. We can access that same Helper today. He (the Holy Spirit), keeps us connected to God even when we keep being unplugged from our communities.

Dear Lord, help me stay connected to You despite all the changes going on around me. Thank You for giving us Your Holy Spirit to guide and encourage us. Amen.

DAY 112

PSALM 104:19–35;
LUKE 15:11–31

Global communication

**'How many are your works, O LORD!
In wisdom you made them all; the earth
is full of your creatures.' (Psa. 104:24)**

This second half of Psalm 104 describes the order of things: how God has set the world in motion and how all things in nature work in their right seasons. Look at verse 25, 'There is the sea, vast and spacious, teeming with creatures beyond number ...' Have you ever been snorkelling or scuba diving? It's incredible just how much beauty and variety exists beneath the waters. The Disney film *Finding Nemo*, shows the Barrier Reef in glorious technicolor, but in real life it is even more amazing. The film follows the search of a daddy fish across the ocean to find his lost son – an echo of the story that Jesus told in Luke 15, of the prodigal son.

When we are separated from our loved ones by many miles, it's comforting to know that our heavenly Father is always ready to 'meet' with them and us. When we pray to the God who set the world in motion and connect with Him, so our prayers can cross the miles and connect with those we love. Our souls can be lifted as we find ways to praise the Lord, and I know my husband in Afghanistan felt more sustained by God as I prayed for him. To help him feel more connected to us, sometimes I would email him the prayers that our boys said before bed. Despite the fact that we were separated by great oceans, through prayer we could still link up, both to each other and to our great God who is above all and sustains all.

Dear Lord, when we are separated from our loved ones, help us to find ways of being connected to one another and to You. Amen.

DAY 113

PSALM 105:1–23;
MATTHEW 28:20

Our first posting was to Germany. Everything in those first two years was new and the learning curve was bigger than I had ever experienced before. I felt an exile in a foreign culture. My husband did two tours in those two years so there were many things I had to find the courage to do on my own for the very first time. I knew I could either forget God and try and go it alone *or* I could trust Him to see me through each challenging (and sometimes frightening!) situation. I looked back over my life, remembered how God had been my guide and strength and that He had never failed me, and knew I could go forward trusting that He would get me through once again.

The psalmist recounts some amazing interventions by God in history as He led His people on a journey. They had some hard, even very hard, times exiled

Remember, remember

DAY 114

PSALM 105:24–45;
JOHN 1

Order out of chaos

in different countries (sound familiar?) experiencing the challenges and difficulties associated with that. But God was their guide through it all. He never gave up on them or abandoned them. He knew the bigger picture and saw them through. May I encourage you to take some time to sit quietly and reflect over your life – remembering how God has protected, guided and provided for you. Then, whatever your situation, be assured that God is still there and wanting to continue to walk with you.

---

*My Father and my God, help me to follow
the example of the psalmist and remember
Your faithfulness to me. Enable me to
move forward knowing You are in my
todays and my tomorrows. Thank You.
Amen.*

I sat in the lounge today watching my son play 'armies'. The son of a soldier, he is fascinated by tanks, helicopters and guns. I have long given up on banning these toys from our home and concentrate instead on using every opportunity to deplore the need for violence and to stress that the God-given role of the Military is to bring order where there is chaos. I watched whilst a battle unfolded and my son guided missiles and tanks in slow motion with unerring accuracy to create the outcome he had chosen. Everything was stage-managed, nothing happened by chance.

As I look at the second half of Psalm 105, throughout it all I see the hand of God moving with unerring accuracy to ensure the outcomes He has decided. He is the one who determines the birth-rate, who sends darkness, turns water to blood, releases plagues of gnats, frogs, flies and

locusts. He is the one who brings Israel out of Egypt and establishes them in their own land that so His people might keep His precepts and obey His laws. In this, their priestly role was to model His kingdom to all nations (1 Pet. 2:5). I am struck simultaneously by the Almighty-ness of God who is able to stage-manage the whole of creation and the awesome humility of the same God who came to earth as a baby, born in a stable to show us the way to Himself. God became man; or as Genie in Disney's 1992 film *Aladdin* puts it, 'Phenomenal cosmic powers ... itty bitty living space.'

---

*O God, thank You for Your extraordinary
gift of coming to earth to live among us
rather than stage-managing everything
from heaven. Amen.*

DAY 115

Pride before a fall

'They forgot the God who saved them, who had done great things in Egypt.' (Psa.106:21)

It is so easy in a military environment to fall into the trap of striving to be self-sufficient, independent and in control. We can sometimes feel as if we are surrounded on all sides by people who appear to be ultra-confident, capable and self-sufficient.

The first half of Psalm 106 is a great warning of what happens if we allow ourselves to fall into this trap and let our pride get in the way of our relationship with God. Pride blinds us to the Lord's blessings and it blocks our memory of all the great things He has done. Aspiring to what we encounter around us can be very misleading and may take us away from God when He wants us to draw closer. In the Bible this behaviour is called 'foolishness' and many of the proverbs like the one in today's cross reference, warn us that pride is usually followed by disgrace.

Conversely, the most neglected virtue in military circles, humility, is described throughout Scripture as a key to true wisdom. Humility is not seeing yourself as less than you are; it is seeing yourself the way *Christ* sees you. Pride is an area that I definitely need some help with – what about you? This psalm is a great reminder and encouragement to keep our pride at bay.

Dear Father, don't let my pride get in the way of my relationship with You. Help me to give thanks for Your blessings and to remember that Your love endures forever. Give me true humility in all my thinking and allow me to see myself through Your eyes. Amen.

DAY 116

This second half of Psalm 106 makes for sombre reading. It catalogues all the ways in which God's people disobeyed His orders. These rules were designed to keep God's people safe but, because the people ignored them, they had to face the consequences of their actions and they experienced God's punishment and anger. Our lives are full of rules and laws. There are the obvious ones, those we have grown up with – don't steal, don't murder, don't break the speed limit; then there are those we have to learn when we move to a foreign country. When I lived in Germany I had to obey new rules; make sure your rubbish goes in the right bin; only cross the road at a recognised crossing; don't hang your washing out on Sunday!

In the Military there are countless rules and orders to follow, they often affect the activities of the whole family,

Following orders

'They grumbled in their tents and did not obey the Lord.' (Psa. 106:25)

not just the Service man or woman. We may see the point in some of these orders but so many of them appear senseless as we see things from our own perspective and aren't shown the valid reasons why they are there. The temptation to ignore them and 'grumble in our tents' is great! But God calls on us to be obedient, not only to the laws of the land but also to His laws. The Israelites defied God's laws and suffered the consequences. Yet, at the end of the psalm, God hears their pain and distress and forgives 'out of his great love' (Psa. 106:45).

It is because of His great love that we can receive forgiveness when we mess up.

DAY 117

PSALM 107:1–22;
2 CORINTHIANS 4:6

Much of officer training involves leadership training in the field. I hated these 'leads'. Whilst I had no problems briefing, delegating or encouraging, many of the leads were technical in nature (I am not!) and I couldn't solve them. Worse, I wasn't allowed to use my team to help solve the problem; I was expected to solve it myself. I think I was deliberately given these types of leads as this was my weak area, but, instead of improving, I just felt stupid and my performance worsened. Fortunately, with God, we are never left alone to solve our problems. We are free to approach Him with a seemingly unsolvable problem and He will lead us to a solution.

In today's reading the psalmist identifies three groups of people who found themselves in various trying circumstances. In each case, they cried

Keeping the faith

'Let them give thanks to the Lord … for he breaks down gates of bronze and cuts through bars of iron.' (Psa. 107:15–16)

out to the Lord in their trouble and He was faithful in meeting their needs. The psalmist then encouraged them to give thanks to the Lord for His faithful love. Notice, that as soon as they turned their eyes upon the Lord and focused on Him, then His light dawned in their particular circumstances, and a solution was found!

If we let Him, God can use our costly experiences to mould and shape us and bring us into a better relationship with Him. Oysters get tiny particles of grit in their shells, which irritate their bodies. The oyster exudes a sticky substance around the source of the irritation to make it more comfortable; eventually a beautiful and treasured pearl is produced – but it was costly to the oyster.

Lord, help me to see Your purposes in all circumstances. Amen.

DAY 118

PSALM 107:23–43;
1 JOHN 5:1–5

Train hard, fight easy

**'Whoever is wise, let him heed these things
and consider the great love of the Lord.'**
(Psa. 107:43)

DAY 119

PSALM 108;
GENESIS 1

If there was one thing I found extremely tedious during my time in the RAF, it was keeping my kit up to standard, especially polishing my shoes. I could never attain that glass-like quality on leather, no matter how hard I tried. They were never that comfortable either which made it even more of a chore. I've often thought how rules and regulations within the Military can appear ridiculously petty or far too strict especially when they don't seem to make much sense. For me, they added extra burdens to my busy schedule.

I have also noticed how the same attitude can sometimes affect the way that many of us relate to God. We can think of him as a petty taskmaster with a big rule book. As I read the Old Testament I see that the Israelites took this view on many occasions, but then found themselves in great difficulties. They thought they knew best but realised eventually that obeying God actually enabled them to live more contented lives.

Just as the Military's rules and regulations help prepare and train us to survive in hostile environments, there is purpose in all of God's instructions too. But there is one big difference with God: His commands are not 'burdensome' (1 John 5:3). Why not? Because Jesus has already fulfilled all of God's commands for us. A friend once said to me, 'God is to be enjoyed not endured'. So the question is, are you enduring God the way you endure a kit inspection or are you enjoying Him today?

What things do you really enjoy? Going for a country walk, meeting friends, reading a good book by a roaring fire? Why not consciously invite God's presence to be with you the next time you are having fun.

When we are in the car, there is a game my youngest likes to play: 'If you were an animal/bird/fish which animal/bird/fish would you be?' This often leads to great discussion because invariably someone will say 'dolphin', which leads to the question of whether a dolphin is a fish or an animal. My eldest has now got wise to this game and answers every question with, 'Whatever God would want me to be.' This rather trite answer holds a lot of lessons for all of us. How many of us look in the mirror and pick faults with ourselves? As women, we are seldom satisfied with our shape. 'If only I could take a bit off here and put it there; I'm too short … too tall … too fat … too thin.'

We always seem to want what we don't have. Perhaps that is why the psalmist 'harps' on and on about giving thanks to God in this psalm. We are told in Genesis

Who am I?

'So God created man in his own image, in the image of God he created him; male and female he created them.'
(Gen. 1:27)

that we have been made in the image of God, that we are as God made us. Yes, we should take care of our bodies and not fill them with too much chocolate or alcohol, but our basic shape and features have been made by God. God doesn't make mistakes so we need to accept ourselves as we are. Perhaps then we will feel 'at home' in our bodies; we will become more content and accepting, not just with ourselves but with people around us as well.

Lord, please help me to see Your image in me and in people around me. Help me to accept myself for who I am. Thank You for making me in Your image. Amen.

DAY 120

PSALM 109;
ROMANS 12:17–21

You can tell from this psalm how fed up David is with people accusing him and letting him down. People will always do this, and still today our friends or families can still hurt us. Have you ever had neighbours or friends suddenly turn on you after all your kindness towards them? Although at no point in this psalm does David tell God it's His fault (he still manages to praise God and describes himself as a man of prayer), he really wants some good retribution! Oh yes, David wants these evil men repaid for their deeds in all manner of horrible ways!

However, since Jesus came, God is not in the business of helping us 'get back' at our enemies, but loving them, despite our hurts. In Romans 12:17–21 we are told not to take revenge or repay evil for evil, and that's hard! But Jesus came to show us how to love like God loves, and He left us His

An eye for an eye?

'... I am poor and needy, and my heart is wounded within me.' (Psa. 109:22)

Holy Spirit to dwell within us to change our hearts.

I remember being badly let down by a friend who was going to flat-share with me, leaving me to pay the whole rent. I was seething as I couldn't afford it. But God spoke to me through a verse in Luke 6:29 about giving your shirt to someone too, even when they've only asked for your coat! I knew I could no longer stay angry with my friend, and asked God to help me forgive her, and my money issues soon worked out as well!

Lord Jesus, help me to have love for the people who have hurt and let me down. Teach me to love them the way You do. Amen.

DAY 121

PSALM 110;
EPHESIANS 6:10–20

Soldiers for Christ

'Your troops will be willing on your day of battle. Arrayed in holy majesty, from the womb of the dawn you will receive the dew of your youth.' (Psa. 110:3)

Smash! There was a terrifying crunch as a brick hit the Landrover windscreen, sending fragments of glass like tiny needles flying into my face. We were on the outskirts of Skopje in Macedonia, driving back to our hilltop site. Shower facilities at our site were rudimentary, so I'd just had a lovely hot shower at the HQ, and stupidly had been applying some face cream at the time. I was now covered in glass, which was stuck to the cream, as well as in my eyes and mouth. On this occasion I was definitely unprepared, unlike God's troops in today's psalm.

Ephesians 6:12 reminds me that there is a bigger battle all of us are fighting daily – one that is 'not against flesh and blood but against the rulers, against the authorities, against the powers of this dark world and against the spiritual forces of evil in the heavenly realms'. The question we need to ask is – are we well-trained and ready for the spiritual battle? Are we willing to fight on the day of battle, wearing the spiritual body armour that God provides? I truly believe that God intervened that day and protected me from horrific injuries. Shortly afterwards, all vehicles were fitted with mesh covers. I was even able to see the humourous side despite the aftershock when, back at base my Sergeant complimented me on my choice of moisturiser whilst patiently picking the minute glass shards out of my skin!

Lord, help me to use the spiritual body armour You have provided so that when I face the enemy I am well prepared, willing and able to face him in Your strength and not my own. Amen.

DAY 122

PSALM 111;
1 JOHN 4:18

'OK then, I'll meet you in the car park by the guardroom at 09:20 and make sure you are not late!' The telephone connection was cut and I found myself wondering what would happen if I couldn't get there on time. 'Be here', 'wear this', 'don't do that' were catch phrases when I was the girlfriend of an officer cadet at Sandhurst. Seeing the Army through his eyes I began to imagine that there was God – and then there was the Platoon Commander! I became afraid of doing something wrong whenever I visited Sandhurst. After a parade one day I found myself chatting with a small group of officer cadets, when a smart uniformed Captain came and introduced himself, 'Hello, we haven't met before. My name's Matthew.' I became aware of the instant silence and the half-opened mouths of the others around me. Surely, this wasn't

DAY 123

PSALM 112;
2 TIMOTHY 1:7

Perfectly loved

'The fear of the Lord is the beginning of wisdom; all who follow his precepts have good understanding.' (Psa. 111:10)

the bogey-man I'd been led to expect! I realised I had no need to fear this (rather charming) man, as his punishments were reserved only for those he disciplined.

Verse 10 says that the 'fear of the Lord is the beginning of wisdom'. It is indeed wise to start by fearing Almighty God who has the power to eternally save or condemn. But it shouldn't end there as God offers us a new relationship, the love of a father towards his precious child. This relationship negates the need for anxious dread, replacing it with the desire to keep His rules not just because they make sense, but more importantly, because it pleases the One who loves us so completely and plans only good for us.

Lord, let me see, know and love You more deeply as my Father. Amen.

No fear!

'He will have no fear of bad news; his heart is steadfast, trusting in the Lord.' (Psa. 112:7)

This psalm continues where we left off yesterday. It speaks of the two types of 'fear'. Firstly, the fear of the Lord – a holy fear – a mixture of delight, respect and awe. Secondly, the type of fear we are more familiar with: dread, anxiety and worry. Verse 7 says a man (or woman!) who fears God is blessed, but even more wonderful than that, has NO fear of bad news because their heart is secure. That's a hard one to live out in a warzone. It can even be hard when we are the one who is left behind; of course we will fear *that* phone call.

A rock in a storm is unmoved by the waves crashing around it – our hearts can be like that when we trust in God. I have found that the only way to counterbalance the fear of death is by regularly reading this psalm and others too, putting my husband's name in the place of 'you' or 'I'. Doing this replaces natural fear with love and respect for God. I have also found that listening regularly to words of truth in worship songs helps, as does *not* listening to fearful words that so many news articles bring! When we are tired, lonely or bored, our fears get more of a foothold. I need to be disciplined to get to bed early and eat regularly, as well as plan fun girls' nights-in. When I stay 'in shape' like this, I don't dwell as much on the 'maybes' that give way to fear.

Father God, thank You that Your perfect love drives out fear. Please help me to delight in You so that my heart will not be fearful. Amen.

DAY 124

A spiritual family

'He settles the barren woman in her home as a happy mother of children.' (Psa. 113:9)

I have witnessed the pain and isolation of barrenness in two friends in recent years. The first friend was unable to conceive for gynaecological reasons; the second had simply never met Mr Right. Now she is too old to have children. Both experienced a longing and a grief, a feeling of being incomplete without a family of their own. I have seen a similar longing in many military folk for a spiritual family, normally developed by worshipping with the same church over many years. It can be hard to experience this when faced with the constant upheaval of a military lifestyle. As today's readings remind us, God knows about these desires – indeed they are there because of the way He has designed us – and He can meet those needs, sometimes miraculously.

For me, He has met this need for a spiritual family through the Armed Forces' Christian Union. Like many others, I have been hugely blessed by the love and support given and received by people of all ages. My children have experienced the 'rooted-ness' of growing up alongside friends; and they are true friends even though they only see each other infrequently at weekends, 'Easter Camp' and other AFCU gatherings. My husband and I have benefited from the wisdom, mentoring and prayer cover of some of the older members. Truly, God can be praised in the words of this psalm, 'From the rising of the sun to the place where it sets' (v.3), for He brings forth fruit from places of barrenness.

Father God, today I bring before You my own unfulfilled needs. I praise You that You know them and can meet them. I entrust them again to You today. Amen.

DAY 125

I was once accused of stealing some dinner money. At the time, I was not eight years old but twenty-eight – and I was the teacher! The injustice of the accusation and the venom that accompanied it was disproportionate to both the occasion and the paltry sum of money involved. Over the next few weeks and months I would take care to avoid private conversation with the parents who accused me and, in the years that followed, I would remember every detail of that and other encounters. Of course, the issues were bigger than the missing £2.81 but this catalyst caused my heart to become hardened in a small yet insidious way and I became wary, cautious and yes, rather bitter. This affected my behaviour towards the people involved. While initially it protected me from further hurt, it created a barrier which prevented me from ever attempting to

Stony hearts

'Tremble, O earth, at the presence of the Lord … who turned the rock into a pool, the hard rock into springs of water.' (Psa. 114:7–8)

DAY 126

PSALM 115;
ZECHARIAH 10:12

Come out of hiding!

'You who fear him, trust in the LORD – he is their help and shield.' (Psa. 115:11)

rebuild the relationship. My heart and responses also became a bit harder towards God as self-righteousness took hold and prevented me from being able to forgive those who had accused me and therefore to really concentrate in prayer.

Of course, this is only a trivial example of unforgiveness; usually the injustices perpetrated against us are much more serious and the result devastatingly destructive. Still, the only solution, whatever the size, is to take it to Jesus. He alone has the ability to take our hearts of stone and replace them with a heart of flesh. Although a flesh heart can bruise more easily, it is also softer towards God and more receptive to the infilling of His Holy Spirit.

Where is your heart stony today? Ask Him to bring forth His springs of living water from the rock.

Who remembers hiding under the quilt when it thundered? Or hiding behind the settee when *Dr Who* was on TV? Maybe I am just showing my age but, however old we are, we often try and hide behind flimsy things when we are worried or frightened. When life is too hard to face, we hide in our bedrooms or our homes. When a difficult conversation needs to be had or a letter written, when we really should go to the Wives' Club meeting for the sake of the other wives, we can become very busy doing other 'important' things. We hide behind our busy lives rather than face that mountain, and yet it still hangs over us, getting bigger and more frightening the longer we leave it.

I have found that there is something I can do that will enable me to face all those difficult issues. First of all, I need to talk to God about it and ask for His

wisdom and strength, and then I need to act – to go out, trusting that God *does* listen and *answers* these prayers. I need to face these fearful times with confidence, knowing that I am not alone.

Trust in the Lord. He is your help and your shield. He won't just throw you a cushion to hide behind; He will walk by your side and hold a whopping great shield over you!

Lord, I bring to You all the difficult things I am facing today. Please show me what I should do. I ask that You will be with me as I face the things that bother me and hold a shield over me in every situation. Amen.

DAY 127

PSALM 116;
EPHESIANS 2:6–10

God's posting order

'I love the LORD, because He hears my voice *and* my supplications. Because He has inclined His ear to me, therefore I shall call *upon Him* as long as I live.'
(Psa. 116:1–2, NASB)

DAY 128

PSALM 117;
ISAIAH 25:1

'Oh Lord, not again!' I had been pouring out my frustrations, sadness and anger to God for several months as I came to terms with moving overseas again. I'd had four happy years in one place where I attended a lively church, made good friends and had a job I loved. Once more I was being asked to give it up and start again. I had tried to think of ways around going, but knew deep in my heart I should be accompanying my husband. During this adjustment phase, my daughter and I attended a women's Christian conference. At the end of the morning session, the organisers shared some words which they felt God had given them. I was looking forward to lunch and wasn't expecting anything relevant to me. Then it happened! It was as if no one else was there and the words spoken from the front were from God speaking directly to

me. He told me He had seen all my hopes, disappointments and struggles following my husband. He had been with me all the time. He told me to trust Him and to look to Him for support and worth.

Well, who was I to question God's plans? Amazingly, once I made the commitment to continue to move with my husband, I had an overwhelming sense of peace. Once there, were my fears realised? No. Were there struggles? Yes. But was it the right place for me to be? Of course! But then God knew that already!

Lord Jesus, we thank You that You know what is best for us. Please help us to accept Your plans for our lives and joyfully follow them. Amen.

Four weeks before my husband was due to be posted back to the UK, we still didn't have a quarter. We had just spent a year with him mostly away on operations and were looking forward to having some settled family life. Now it could be several more months before we were all together. We sent an urgent prayer request to friends and family. We had already prayed that God would put us where He wanted us. There were no houses at the actual base, so the housing department was looking for a hiring and asked us to travel over to view the options. So, as it was half term, our whole family made an unplanned trip to the UK.

Once there, we learnt that nothing had been arranged, but the housing agency promised to 'find something in the next two days'. We tried to stay calm and trust that God was in control. The day before

Marvellous things!

'O Lord you are my God; I will exalt you and praise your name, for in perfect faithfulness you have done marvellous things, things planned long ago.'
(Isa. 25:1)

DAY 129

PSALM 118;
ISAIAH 12

God is for me

'The Lord is with me; I will not be afraid. What can man do to me?' (Psa. 118:6)

we were due to return, the agency still hadn't found anything. My husband phoned the housing department again and offered to take anything suitable even if it meant commuting. They said that a quarter had, unexpectedly, just become available! Would we like to see it? It was the loveliest house we had ever lived in and our time there was really special. Our wait taught us that we need to trust God, for He loves us more than we can imagine and does marvellous things for us. Praise the Lord!

Praise You, Lord, that You love us and delight in doing marvellous things for us! Help us to trust You more and more. Amen.

A couple of weeks after moving into our first married quarter, my husband made a passing comment which didn't go down well with some of the people on the street. The result was that half our neighbours blanked us for the remainder of the tour. Patch life is not always easy; it is a bit like living in the office – you are with the same people day and night. First impressions can count for so much and we so often just want to blend in and get on.

Blending in as a Christian can be tricky though. It can result in compromise of ourselves and ultimately God; a high price to pay for a comfortable life. Sometimes the patch can feel like the hostile land of Psalm 118. And we can feel alone or intimidated. Verse 6 exhorts us not to be afraid. Our greatest security is in God who is *for us*. This psalm encourages us by reminding us that God

is always with us. So we do not need to be afraid of what our neighbours may do or say. It may still not be pleasant, but God will give us the strength and He will carry the burden of our troubles. After all, He has dealt with bigger issues and also cares deeply for things that are much smaller (see Matt. 10:29). Let us keep putting our trust in Him as we refuse to compromise but instead seek His love and comfort through it all.

Use the words in Isaiah 12 as your own prayer of praise and declaration of trust in God today. Pray for joy as you 'draw water from the wells of salvation' (v.3).

DAY 130

Combating anxiety

'I run in the path of your commands, for you have set my heart free.' (Psa. 119:32)

I'm the kind of person who likes her 'ducks in a row' and therefore life can become stressful for me when I have to live with uncertainty, change or things appearing to be out of control. During these times I can become easily anxious, and so, in God's great wisdom, He called me into the Navy and gave me a Naval husband with all the change and moving around that entails.

Living at sea for extended periods of time with no means of escape, mainly surrounded only by men, I have often felt at my most anxious, my most lonely and my most vulnerable. In verse 32 of today's psalm, we see that when we are in the 'path' of God's commands, our heart is set free. For me, this has meant that, to survive Naval life, I have needed to run towards God and into His path continually – staying close to His Word,

remembering that His Word is truth (v.43) and seeking Him and the guidance and comfort of the Holy Spirit through my Quiet Times. Only when I have done this, do I feel my anxiety lift and a sense of peace and perspective comes.

In Phillipians 4:6–7 (my life-verse!) we read that we are not to be anxious about anything but, through offering our prayer needs to God – literally, pouring out our heart – we will have peace, the opposite of anxiety. This doesn't mean that I don't still get anxious but as time has gone on I find I am learning to give my anxieties to God and don't allow them to utterly consume me.

Dear Lord, help me to trust You – completely. Amen.

DAY 131

One of the more challenging decisions I have had to face was whether to move when my husband was posted to Washington DC. I didn't want to go! At the time we had two small children and living in the UK gave me close access to my family and friends – and I also knew that a move like this could have a negative impact on my career. The move, therefore, was costly, not least because throughout the posting I experienced loneliness and isolation.

The turning point for me came when I finally found a church which had excellent teaching. I began to learn the delight of obeying God. How often do we do this, especially when facing difficult decisions? Looking back, I can see that God was faithful to His Word and His promises as I held fast to His statutes (Psa. 119:31). By sacrificing my will for His, I gained much

All our tomorrows

'Let me live that I may praise you,
and may your laws sustain me.'
(Psa. 119:175)

calling out to God for support, protection and salvation. Here we see that he rises before dawn and stays awake long into the night to meditate on God's Word. He declares God's Word as truth and praises Him for His righteousness. How often when facing difficult tomorrows do we eagerly and urgently turn to God in praise and prayer? It is tempting to look for human solutions and come to God as a last resort. But God wants us to begin by coming to Him, so that He can give us peace and strength. This will help us prepare for every trial.

Dear Lord, keep us focused on You and following Your Word as we prepare for the tomorrows that You have ordained for us. Amen.

DAY 135

PSALM 120;
GALATIANS 5:26

In the Military we often end up living in locations we would not choose for ourselves. It is difficult to feel unique or individual in the military environment. Our husbands wear the same uniforms; our houses look the same; sometimes we even end up buying clothes from the same catalogue! We live so closely we know most of the details about the family next door. It seems almost impossible not to compare ourselves with our neighbours – do I dress as well as that wife? Are our holidays as exciting? Are our kids doing as well as theirs? Have we managed to make our quarter look unique? Do we have a smarter car? Does my husband have a higher rank? Are we better?

As normal human beings it is so difficult not to ask these questions and make comparisons; as children of God these are questions that should not

Unique even in uniform!

'How I suffer in far-off Meshech. It pains
me to live in distant Kedar. I am tired
of living among people who hate peace.'
(Psa. 120:5–6, NLT)

bother us. (I know that is easier said than done!) But, in God's love we find security. We shouldn't need the affirmation and approval of our neighbour because we are all equal and yet unique in God's eyes. As Psalm 139:15 says, God 'wove' us together in our mother's womb. No one knows or loves us more. God has so much for us. No matter where we are living or who our neighbours are, God loves us and sees each of us as an individual. We just need to relax and revel in God's love for us.

Dear God, please help me to realise my worth in You. Help me to accept it and live it out in my life – wherever I find myself living. Amen.

DAY 136

PSALM 121;
HEBREWS 13:6

Buddy up

**'I lift up my eyes to the hills –
where does my help come from?'**
(Psa. 121:1)

DAY 137

PSALM 122;
HEBREWS 10:24–25

So often when we are faced with fear, a trial, test or affliction, we choose to look down in self-pity or around at others rather than gazing upward to God for His help. Downtown Naples, Italy, is not the safest place for a woman to be by herself, especially at night. I was stationed there as a young Wren and regularly travelled from the NATO base to the US Christian Servicemen's Centre (CSC) downtown. I prayed for God's protection every time I had to travel alone.

I remember on one particular occasion, after attending a wedding in Capri, feeling extremely vulnerable as I was not dressed in my normal 'blend in' mode of no jewellery and a carrier bag instead of a handbag; I was wearing a suit, jewellery and – worst of all – sporting the forbidden handbag! Needing to walk from the hydrofoil in Fleet Landing, to the

CSC, I prayed for God's protection. Two US sailors suddenly appeared so I decided to move in close behind and follow them. Amazingly, they also were also going to the CSC. On the stairs to the Centre they told me that they had heard about the dangers in Naples and had felt rather nervous because I was following them! They found the whole thing amusing when I told them the reason why. Naples taught me many lessons about trusting totally in God for His help and protection.

The Lord is our shade or 'shadow'. Just as our shadow goes everywhere with us, God shadows us at all times and in all circumstances, He is our refuge and protection.

Lord, remind us to always look up to You for our protection and help. Amen.

I admit to finding this verse from Psalm 122 difficult these days. I used to attend a very lively Anglican church that I looked forward to going to week by week, and genuinely rejoiced when it was time for church on Sunday, morning and evening, and again on Tuesday for the mid-week prayer meeting. There was an air of expectation, not quite knowing what God was going to do in our midst that week. After I joined the Army however, things became so much more difficult as lively churches were harder to find and fellowship with other Christians often hard to establish due to frequent postings.

Today's passage from Hebrews exhorts us not to give up meeting together, and I believe that means that we need to go to church even if it doesn't quite give us the buzz that we would like, and that we should make it a priority over the football

DAY 138

PSALM 123;
MARK 6:31

Looking forward to church?

**'I rejoiced with those who said to me,
"Let us go to the house of the Lord."'**
(Psa. 122:1)

or sleeping-in or whatever else we are tempted to do at the time of the Sunday service. It also means that we need to find time to meet other Christians through a prayer meeting, Bible Study group or other fellowship group during the week. Hebrews 10:25 tells us to meet together to 'encourage one another'. Does your presence in church or at the Bible Study encourage the padre or the leader of the group? Do you go in order to encourage others, or do you decline to attend because you don't personally get anything out of it?

Dear Lord, forgive me when I don't want to go to church. Spur me on to determine to meet with other Christians in order to encourage them. Amen.

Psalm 123 is known as 'A Pilgrim's Song'. In the Military, our journey of faith is sometimes hard and lonely. Today, for a change, let's mediate on a poem I once wrote which encourages us to turn aside from the busyness of life and meet with Jesus:

Come aside by yourselves to a deserted
place and rest awhile.
The road is hard and long;
robbers prowl by the wayside
waiting to steal My peace from you.
The battle is fierce;
the enemy strong.
Don't forget where you belong.
Stand aside – away from the crowd
and rest in Me – don't be too proud.
Fight on alone, you know you will fail.
Only I have the strength;
only I will prevail.
Let Me fight by your side,

Turn aside and rest

**'I look to you, heaven-dwelling God,
look up to you for help.'**
(Psa. 123:1, *The Message*)

let Me take life's strain.
Rest in Me when it's tough –
your strength to regain.
Come aside by yourself
from the trouble and strife;
rest with Me for a while –
I AM the Truth and your Life.

Lord God, would You help me to put aside the distractions of the world and make space to rest in You and Your love for me. Amen.

DAY 139

PSALM 124;
JOSHUA 5:13–14

Taking sides

'Our help comes from the Lord, who made heaven and earth.' (Psa. 124:8, GNB)

God must be on our side. We are right after all! How many wars and battles have been fought with each side believing they are in the right? How many tiffs have we had, convinced that we have been right? I was involved in a legal conflict, convinced that I was right and so reassured that God was on 'my' side and everything would go my way in the end. Right must prevail after all!

I recently read some verses from Joshua 5 and they really made me stop and think. How often do we go through life convinced that our viewpoint and not the Army's or the CO's is the right one and so God must agree with us and will fight with us to get the result we want in the end? In Psalm 124, the Israelites gave thanks to God because He had been on their side and they had won a great battle. In the verses from Joshua, the angel of

the Lord stated he wasn't on anyone's side; he had come as the commander of the army of the Lord. This doesn't mean that the Israelites were wrong in believing God was fighting for them – rather their perspective was misplaced. God fought for them because they were obeying His commands. They came into line with God rather than God coming over to their side. Just so, we need to bring our conflicts to God and ask Him to show us His perspective on the situation and then align our views to His. This won't be easy but God will help us to do it.

Lord, please show me things from Your perspective. Amen.

DAY 140

PSALM 125;
2 CORINTHIANS 4:16–18

We are surrounded by uncertainty on a daily basis – everything from 'Is it going to rain?' to 'What will the next posting be?' These things can bring concern and worry. Sometimes we go through periods when our worries and stresses mount up until we feel snowed-under and there seems to be no 'light at the end of the tunnel'. When this happens it is very easy to feel that everything is outside our control. Indeed, there are times when I have felt like a piece of flotsam tossed around on a wave, unable to take a direct course or make any progress in any direction.

Psalm 125:2 says, 'As the mountains surround Jerusalem, so the Lord surrounds his people both now and for evermore'. It is a wonderful reassurance to know that as we trust in the Lord, He will encircle us just like the mountains

Strength like a mountain

'Those who trust in the LORD are like Mount Zion, which cannot be shaken but endures forever.' (Psa. 125:1)

DAY 141

PSALM 126;
MARK 8:34

'Those who sow in tears will reap with songs of joy. He who goes out weeping carrying seed to sow, will return with songs of joy carrying sheaves with him.' (Psa. 126:5–6)

encircle Jerusalem. We can know that we are making progress in the right direction, even if the direction of travel feels unclear. A desire to be in control only serves to create worry and stress. Paul exhorts us to 'fix our eyes not on what is seen, but on what is unseen' (2 Cor. 4:18) – the presence of the Lord encircling and enfolding us. If we trust in the Lord, He will take care of us, and the strength that He gives us is like a mountain which cannot be shaken.

Dear Lord, help me to trust You in all things, remembering that if I try to take control of them it will lead to disappointment and anxiety, but to have faith in You is like an unshakable mountain that endures forever. Amen.

After seventeen years of marriage and fourteen house moves, you would think that moving would be easy for me. However, I don't move well and each move feels costly and sacrificial as I say goodbye to the friends I've made and the church family of which I've been a part. During the early months of settling down, I often feel tearful and lacking in joy – reaching out to others can be the last thing on my mind.

It is said that having self on the mind all the time ensures a miserable life, but in a culture of 'me-ism' we can often find that this is just what we are drawn to do, when in a place of need. Today's psalm, however, shows us that our joy will return if we turn our attention away from ourselves and sow blessing into the lives of others. God's 'Harvest Law' says that when we give sacrificially, we will reap abundant

blessings. The seeds we have to sow could be showing kindness, generosity, love and friendship, or the sacrificial giving of our time and resources to others.

Recently, God asked me to do something that would take up precious time that I had set aside for packing and preparing for moving. It felt costly. However, God more than made up for it. When we arrived at our new posting I had provision that I'd not expected and the move turned out to be one of our easiest. The promise was fulfilled and I had joy by the sheaf-full!

Dear Lord, deliver me from self-centredness and help me to be always willing to sow into the lives of others, whatever the cost to myself. Amen.

DAY 142

PSALM 127;
HAGGAI 2:19

Do you ever feel like you are trying to achieve something or be someone that you're not? I have experienced this most as a servicewoman in the RAF. Adultery, heavy drinking, gossiping etc, are accepted ways of life to many. Your career can be judged on how sociable you are. I am ashamed to say that I used to partake in much of this behaviour. Why? Because I wanted to fit in and be successful. I drank, partied and strove to be the best at everything. A lot of effort went into creating a person that I thought would be accepted and successful by worldly standards – exhausting! But meanwhile, I was slowly dying inside. I was climbing the ladder only to realise that it was against the wrong wall.

When I became a Christian, I was driven to my knees in repentance for all that I had done. I had to ask God to help

God's grand design

'Unless the Lord builds the house, its builders labour in vain. Unless the Lord watches over the city, the watchmen stand guard in vain.' (Psa. 127:1)

me put the ladder against the *right* wall and show me what *He* wanted me to build. It has been a painful journey at times, in which many tears have been shed, but it has been one of continuing refinement. God has taught me that when we build what *He* wants us to, we not only draw deep blessing from working on it, but many others are also blessed by the view from that building. What God said to the exiles when they came into line with His will, He says to you also, 'From this day on I will bless you' (Hag. 2:19).

Thank You, Lord, that You are the ultimate architect. Help us to trust in Your perfect plan for us. Amen.

DAY 143

PSALM 128;
PROVERBS 31:10–31

Have you met 'Super-Woman'? I have, in a variety of guises; she bakes, sews her own curtains, gives her children healthy and nutritious snacks, pumps iron, looks immaculate and cleans her own house – all in addition to a full-time paid job outside the home. Then there is the army wife version, who combines all of the above with the ability to have cordon-bleu dinner parties and run the Wives' Club. Or perhaps you have come across the Super-Christian-Woman, who fits in long and meaningful Quiet Times and never shouts at her kids in public!

I have often read about 'Mrs Proverbs 31' and despaired! If it is a blueprint for Christian women then I for one have failed! In my early married life, hearing horror stories of march-outs, I mopped the kitchen floor daily, because I thought that was what all army wives did! The problem with trying

Super-women!

'Blessed are all who fear the Lord, who walk in his ways.' (Psa. 128:1)

to be someone we are not and attempting to live up to our perception of others' expectations, is that eventually we fail. The areas we've neglected while 'keeping up' appearances soon begin to need major maintenance and repair work. God's solution is found again and again in the Bible where real-life stories are told about ordinary people who had a relationship with God. There's no air-brushing, they weren't perfect, but what they did was what the psalmist did: they focused on God, they walked in His ways and as they did, they experienced His blessing. They became not super, but surrendered, and He achieved extraordinary things through ordinary people.

Lord Jesus, help me to surrender myself to You. Please release me from the burden of trying to be super! Amen.

DAY 144

PSALM 129;
2 TIMOTHY 2:9

'Stop biting your nails!' 'Say please!' 'Don't speak with your mouth full!' 'Blow your nose … *on a tissue*!' 'Look both ways!' 'Have you washed your hands?' These phrases are second nature to most mothers. Why do children need years of training to learn good habits and even longer to break bad ones?! And it is not just children! My worst habit is losing my temper, but I do it so easily even though I know it can be destructive to family life.

Living in an enemy-occupied state, the psalmist knew what control and enslavement felt like. With wonderfully picturesque language he writes 'Ploughmen have ploughed my back and made their furrows long' (Psa.129:3). A bad habit can become a real enemy, a tool of Satan, robbing us of life and freedom. But there is always hope and a way out; '… God's word is not chained' (2 Tim. 2:9)

Old habits die hard!

'... the Lord is righteous; he has cut me free from the cords of the wicked.' (Psa. 129:4)

and His desire is always for our freedom to worship and serve Him.

A young army wife once came to an Alpha course running in our home. She could not seem to break her habit of swearing and was finding it embarrassing and unhelpful, especially in front of her small children. A miracle happened as she prayed the simple prayer committing her life to Jesus: all desire to swear left her instantly. God cut her free from the cords of the wicked. For most of us the process of breaking bad habits with God's help is slower, but no less effective. Do you have a bad habit that is enslaving you today? God is righteous; ask Him to break the cords that bind you. He has the power!

Lord, please grant me freedom today. Show me anything that is enslaving me so that I can break free with You. Amen.

DAY 145

Stand firm!

'If you, O LORD, kept a record of sins, O Lord, who could stand? But with you there is forgiveness, therefore you are feared.'
(Psa. 130:3–4)

Moving around within the Armed Forces has given our family the wonderful opportunity to experience a wide range of worship styles at the military churches we have attended. These worship styles have varied from singing the Eucharistic prayer responses to dancing (yes, I said dancing!) around the church. In our present church family, which is run by an Anglican minister, we are called to stand at different times during the service, one of these times being during the Gospel reading.

I had never really fully appreciated this early morning exercise and had wondered if it was devised as a way of keeping us attentive or as a fitness programme for our ageing bodies. Then one Sunday morning our padre enlightened us. He explained that the Early Church stood to pray and praise the Lord as a sign of their risen life in Christ and that, today, we are also claiming this truth as we rise from our pews. We are raised in Christ. What a wonderful truth we are proclaiming every time we stand!

This led me to think that perhaps when we feel daunted and overwhelmed by difficult tasks or even knocked down by stormy situations, it would be good to remember this simple truth. Jesus is *risen* and we are in Him, so let us stand with confidence in our new life in Christ!

Heavenly Father, thank You so very much that Jesus' death paid the price for all my sins, and in His risen life I can stand in Your presence, restored and forgiven. Please Lord, help me to stand firm on this truth today. Amen.

DAY 146

I once felt God saying that He likened my Christian faith at that time to a bunch of artificial flowers; pretty to look at, very similar in appearance to the real thing, but unscented, dead dust-catchers! I was hugely convicted; in fact it was like suddenly seeing a red-light on a motorway. It caused me to slam on my spiritual brakes in order to do some serious soul-searching. I realised that I had become complacent and was trusting in my own abilities and talents rather than Almighty God's resources. I had become 'religious', having 'a form of godliness but denying its power' (2 Tim. 3:5).

This psalm compares the real innocence and complete trust of a satisfied baby with the pseudo-dependence on God many of us grow into after we have been Christians for a while. We pretend we are being like

DAY 147

PSALM 132;
1 CORINTHIANS 9:25

Stop!

**'... I have stilled and quietened my soul;
like a weaned child with its mother ...'
(Psa. 131:2)**

'little children' as we approach God, but in truth are rather proud of our own knowledge and often get entangled in the peripheral 'religious' issues that tend to divide rather than unite believers. This psalm begs me to stop in my tracks today to consider if I can truly say with David in verses 1–2, 'My heart is not proud, O LORD, my eyes are not haughty, I do not concern myself with great matters or things too wonderful for me.' **STOP**! Am I trusting God from a place of complete vulnerability and surrender, or am I trying to live out my 'religious' life from a position of my own strength and knowledge?

Spend time 'stilling your soul in God's presence' today, rejoicing where He sees your dependence on Him and repenting of less perfect areas.

Developing healthy habits

**'I will not enter my house or go to my bed –
I will allow no sleep to my eyes,
no slumber to my eyelids, till I find a
place for the LORD, a dwelling for the
Mighty One of Jacob.' (Psa. 132:3–5)**

As a Junior Troop Commander I used to make a point of letting my soldiers eat first, and, if possible, letting them get some sleep before I did. However, I remember my Squadron Commander insisting that I must get sleep before the soldiers, as they were usually required to carry out certain specific duties for which they had been well practised, whereas I was expected to react to the unexpected, thinking through a problem quickly and devising a plan of action.

It has been scientifically proven that despite lack of sleep, we can carry out routine tasks for which we are well practised, but are much less able to react to new situations. Hence the practice in the Military of conducting many tasks as a routine, repeating them time and time again, to get them established into our sub-consciousness. So it should be with spending time with God, reading His Word and in prayer. We need to find a 'place for the Lord' in our day, so that it becomes second nature to look to Him. The psalmist states he will even go without sleep, so urgent is his quest to find a 'dwelling for the Mighty One'. Not unlike physical exercise (or 'strict training' (1 Cor. 9:25)), once we are in the habit of praying, then it becomes second nature. We may even be able to sleep better too, when we do eventually get to bed!

Lord, thank You for being interested in the good times and the bad, in the big things in our lives and the tiny details. Help me to build up my routine of prayer and my relationship with You. Amen.

DAY 148

PSALM 133;
EPHESIANS 4:7–13

Breaking open the boxes!

'How good and pleasant it is when God's people live together in unity!'
(Psa. 133:1, NIV, 2011)

DAY 149

PSALM 134;
GENESIS 15:5

What does 69.2 cubic metres mean to you? To me, it is the size of my world – the size permitted by the Army whenever we move. My 'world', or all my worldly goods, to be more accurate, has to fit inside a removals lorry. Over the years, I have had to become increasingly inventive about the best way to make everything fit. Sometimes it seems strange to me that, as Christians, we all worship the same God but try to fit Him into our own 'church box'.

God loves to see unity amongst Christians and we see real fruit when we can celebrate our unity despite our differences. Today's short psalm highlights God's pleasure when He sees us working together for the good of His kingdom, 'For there the LORD bestows his blessing; even life for evermore' (v.3). Each house we move into challenges my creativity in arranging our possessions

in a practical as well as aesthetically-pleasing way. In one house I had to tuck the sitting-room rug up behind the sofa to squeeze it in. In another I had to store a favourite bench in the garage. We need this same ingenuity and flexibility when we come to church. Occasionally we might have to put some of our favourite church practices in 'the garage' for a time. True unity is not just about an emotion or a religious doctrine, but about putting aside our differences and focusing on the really important things: loving God and loving each other.

Heavenly Father, help me to use the gifts You have given me for the greater good in a way that unites rather than divides. Amen.

I had the privilege of spending Christmas 2009 with a Logistics Regiment. They spent the majority of their time transporting supplies and equipment between Kuwait and Iraq. The hours were long, the work was repetitive, yet they had to remain ever vigilant, wary of roadside bombs or attacks. As the Padre, I spent Christmas Day holding a Carol Service, giving out presents and serving lunch. However, it was during Christmas night travelling in a Mastiff convoy that I felt most useful and even closest to God.

I found myself sitting with soldiers who felt more able to speak in the darkness about their loved ones and what they were missing during the long hours inside the Mastiff. I, too, was missing my family and the five-minute conversation on the phone that day had only made things worse. Half-way through the night at the

Christmas Day

'Come, bless GOD, all you servants of GOD! You priests of GOD, posted to the nightwatch …' (Psa. 134:1, *The Message*)

border crossing, when we were allowed out for a loo break, I looked up and saw hundreds of stars shining brightly. Surrounded by sand and dust I thought of Abraham and God's promise to him (Gen. 15:5), of how one day he would have as many descendants as he saw stars. God fulfilled that promise, just as He fulfils his promises to each of us. This short psalm reminds us to bless the Lord, because He loves us and wants to bless us. That night as I thought of my own family I remembered that wherever we are around the world and whatever we are doing, we can always look up at the stars and remember God and His promises!

How can I intentionally bless the Lord? Spend time tonight enjoying God's company and telling Him how great He is!

My husband went missing for twelve hours during the first week of his first tour in Bosnia. He was in the last vehicle of a convoy moving to another location and the vehicle in front broke down, and didn't move off with the group. He then tried to find the convoy but took a wrong left turn and got completely lost. He recalled the initial panic inside as he tried to ask directions in another language. Eventually a local from a nearby factory offered to show him the way to the nearest Allied camp.

Whilst on the journey to the camp, the man asked him – in gestures – whether he read the Bible and prayed. My husband said that, within seconds, the latent bubbling fears within him turned to boundless praise. They went on to have a very interesting conversation on the way to the camp where he was kept safe until

Divine rendezvous

'I know that the LORD is great …' (Psa. 135:5)

recovered by his own unit. He never saw the man again.

How great is our God! He can even arrange for us to be protected by angels. Sometimes these divine appointments seem like intrusions into our well-ordered lives. Perhaps the next time it happens we need to ask, is this an interruption or a divine appointment? As we allow our Lord to guide our paths and steps, we will come across unplanned contacts. Every conversation we have will leave an impression on the person we meet. Pray that this impression will be the shape of our Lord.

Lord, let my itinerary not be so full today that You cannot fit in a divine appointment. Amen.

DAY 151

PSALM 136;
LEVITICUS 25:1–7

Life through God's 'window'

**'Thank God, who did it all!
His love never quits!'**
(Psa. 136:26, *The Message*)

DAY 152

PSALM 137;
EPHESIANS 2:19–22

From the high vantage point of the bus, I could see right over the hedges into fields full of ripe wheat and barley. One field, however, had no commercial crop planted in it; instead a carnival of wild flowers, poppies and daisies, competed for space like a bowl of my favourite Italian salad. In the Old Testament, God instructed that the fields should lie fallow once every seven years. This must have been hard to do in a hand-to-mouth subsistence environment, but was ultimately better for the fertility of future crops. It also taught the Jews to rely totally on God rather than their own abilities.

There have been periods in my own life when I have felt frustrated by feelings of unfruitfulness. Times when I have been unable to pursue the career I trained for because of frequent postings, small children and an absentee husband. In

those eras we can feel that we are simply marking time and have little to show in worldly terms. The field of flowers reminded me that to God, the times that can seem the most unfruitful can contain incredible beauty and hidden treasure. Today's beautiful psalm carries the refrain, '*His love never quits.*' God will not fail us. His words and His actions *are* trustworthy and we can put our security in Him, rather than our own abilities to produce a harvest.

Father God, I confess that I find it hard to see Your meaning and purpose in fallow periods of my life. Please help me to trust You completely with the bad times as well as the good, and change my perspective to see the view out of Your window. Amen.

Recently I was looking through photos of the places that my military job has taken me to. I reflected it is hard in the Military sometimes when I am asked to go somewhere that I don't really want to go, or at a time that doesn't feel convenient. Today's psalm was written while the Jews were far from home, having been exiled in Babylon: I can imagine how those displaced Jews must have felt!

Sometimes the very space and way in which I would normally talk to God is taken away too. But, wherever I am stationed, God bathes my soul with His beauty; I just have to look around. I often use this as a starting point for thinking about Him, finding something each day; perhaps a favourite sight, smell or even a certain time, and try to use that to focus on God. One exercise I chose evening: the stark contrast of the tanks

DAY 153

PSALM 138;
PROVERBS 22:5

Sacred space

'How can we sing the songs of the LORD while in a foreign land?' (Psa. 137:4)

silhouetted against the orange sunset sky was stunning. Another time I was blessed to see the local kids come and play with a stray dog on the other side of the wire from me; their innocence and laughter was the perfect antidote to the stressed 'shouty' men of the Operations (planning) tent. In times like these, God reminds us all that we are no longer 'foreigners and strangers, but fellow citizens with God's people' (TNIV) and He is with us – no matter how far we are from home.

If we find ourselves in a situation where our usual Quiet Time with God is not possible, how else might we find Him? How might He be trying to speak to us? Ask Him to show you today.

Being a young officer in my first Mess promised to be exciting and fun; 'plenty of income and no responsibilities', 'cheap food and no washing up'. Surely these times are sent to make up for all the hours spent in a muddy hole on exercise, or eating sand accidentally on operations?

The temptation for a Christian to make small but wrong decisions was massive, and anyone can soon slide unwittingly into a worldly lifestyle. 'All I'm doing is bonding with the guys … unit cohesion and all that.' And it's often the accumulation of lots of little wrong decisions that lead to us falling, not necessarily the major decisions. But, by making decisions too legalistically, we can fall the other way; leaving ourselves lonely and disconnected. With its drinking culture, pressure to conform to unity, and 'work-hard play-hard' ethos, the Military

Mess life

'Though I walk in the midst of trouble, you preserve my life …' (Psa. 138:7)

can be a harsh place in which to thrive as a Christian. I feel like I am walking into trouble on a daily basis, yet the Lord has always provided a way out; a choice for me to make. I find I absolutely *have* to hear the Lord's Word daily in order to ground me and reveal the differences between the world's ways and God's ways. Invariably I make mistakes and mess up. But God forgives my sinful misplaced footsteps.

Father God, sometimes I feel like I live and work in a place surrounded by temptation and my soul is in danger. Father, I praise You that despite this, You will not tempt me beyond what I can bear. Lord, show me these dangers, so that I may choose You over them. Amen.

DAY 154

PSALM 139;
JOB 31:4

The submariner's psalm

'You discern my going out and my lying down; you are familiar with all my ways.'
(Psa. 139:3)

DAY 155

PSALM 140;
MATTHEW 18:20–33

I am sitting on the porch of the OCF Retreat Centre in Pennsylvania surrounded by God's beauty and the enthusiasm of US Military Christians. In the women's group we were asked to take off our masks and be real, not pretending to be the women we thought we should be according to the Bible, but to reveal the women that we truly are, along with all our struggles and weaknesses. A time of deep sharing followed. We quickly recognised the importance of having at least one other woman, and preferably a peer group of women, in similar situations, with whom we can share our struggles and joys. We need friends with whom we can be totally honest, for mutual support and so we can pray together.

God knows us intimately; we cannot wear a mask with Him. From this psalm we learn that God knows our every movement, every thought and even what we are going to say. It is often quoted as the 'Submariner's Psalm' – '… if I make my bed in the depths, you are there' (v.8). We cannot escape from Him, which is both comforting and scary!

This psalm also speaks of the all-creative God and His handiwork in our formation. Regardless of our disability, belief, skin colour or ethnic group, the Lord has been at work as He created each of us. No child is ever a mistake. He sees our every step (see Job 31:4). This impacts the way we perceive others, our own sense of self-worth and our need to wear a mask.

Creator God, thank You for the way You have made us. Help us to be real with You, ourselves and with others. Amen.

'Just leave me alone! If you ever come here again I will call the RMP.' I stared at the closed door aghast; what had I done to cause such a reaction? Over the last few months I had offered and received friendship and then, suddenly, there had been a misunderstanding, a false accusation and the betrayal by a friend. The words cut into my spirit like sharp knives, I rehearsed them in my mind feeling them slice into my self-confidence.

'For if you forgive men when they sin against you, your heavenly Father will also forgive you. But if you do not forgive men their sins, your Father will not forgive your sins (Matt. 6:14–15). I did not want to forgive. I had done nothing wrong, but Jesus' words rang in my mind; I had to forgive even though I did not feel like it. With difficulty (and some days later) I made a choice to forgive and as I did

Deciding to forgive

'They practice the sharp rhetoric of hate and hurt, speak venomous words that maim and kill.' (Psa. 140:3, *The Message*)

so, something happened. I felt free in spite of the pain. I experienced the warm embrace of the Father, and as I began to praise Him another miracle occurred: I experienced His comfort and peace and even His joy restoring my spirit. Perhaps you are struggling to forgive someone today. God is waiting for you with open arms, wanting to lift off the heavy burden you have carried for so long. He longs to set you free and to restore you to a place of peace and joy that is only possible when we worship Him without harbouring any bitterness in our hearts.

Lord Jesus, thank You for forgiving me; please help me to forgive those who hurt me too. Amen.

DAY 156

PSALM 141;
1 THESSALONIANS 5:11

Last month I was at a funeral service for a young man and many lovely tributes were given. It made me wonder how good I am at saying how much I appreciate others. Funerals always make me think, 'Did the person know I thought that about them – while they were alive?' Are you good at saying words that encourage and bless others? It is a biblical gift to be an encourager and it is something I know I need to work on. My mouth can be used to bless or curse others, what a responsibility!

Wouldn't the world be a better place if we all said things that build each other up, perhaps an encouragement, a blessing or a compliment? Let us tell our friends and the people around us that we appreciate them and ask God for His help to bite our tongues when we are tempted to say things we will later regret.

Watch your words

'Set a guard over my mouth, O Lord; keep watch over the door of my lips.' (Psa. 141:3)

Sometimes we need the Lord's help to do this; some people are definitely easier to love than others!

God often gives us friends for a season as we move round various postings. Some we will stay in touch with forever, while with others we might renew friendships at a later date. Yesterday, I unexpectedly received a card from a friend; as I sat down to savour it I thought how nice it was, as nowadays everyone seems to communicate by email. Perhaps you could send a card to someone today, telling them how much you care about them.

Lord God, help me in all that I say today. Bring me alongside those who need to hear Your voice; may my words bless and encourage them. Amen.

DAY 157

A good old moan!

'I pour out my complaint before him, before him I tell him my trouble.' (Psa. 142:2)

I used to wonder why it was that God got so 'fed up' with the Jews moaning their way through the desert after they left Egypt, and yet didn't seem to mind when David complained in psalms like this one. Then I realised that the Jews complained to each other about God, whereas David brought his complaint directly to God. There is a huge difference between grumbling behind someone's back and going straight to that person with a grievance. The latter course of action recognises that the issue can be resolved and addresses the party who has the power to fix it. In Numbers 14, God remarks twice that the people have treated Him with contempt in their grumbling to each other. It is a sobering thought!

Sometimes I catch myself (and others) doing a lot of complaining about various orders or individuals; a posting I didn't want, the long working hours, or a demanding boss. It is true that we are often powerless to challenge the military 'higher powers' about certain aspects of Service life; but, I often fail also to take my complaints to the Highest Power, God Almighty Himself. I know I neglect to ask Him to redress the situation or for His ability to change my heart and perspective. How strange when *He is the One* who can do something about it! It is wonderful to know that we can openly express our anger to Him without fear of reprisal. In return He can address our grievances.

In what areas are you struggling with disappointment and frustration? Bring them to God. Let it all out. Ask Him to change you and those situations.

DAY 158

It was 1973. I had damaged my back and had been in some pain for several months. My best friend had gone to India and my landlord had sold the house in which we had been living and bought a huge new mansion. The atmosphere in the new house was not good. It was damp, cold and had no hot water, and stories I heard suggested that there was spiritual oppression connected to the property. I felt very low, very lonely and disconnected from God; it felt like He was a long way away. I wrote a poem that began:

> I feel I'm in deep darkness, Lord,
> Surrounded by a wall
> Through which no chink of light or love
> Can plumb the depths within ...

As we saw yesterday, the psalmists are brutally honest with God: He wants us to be frank with Him. If you are currently in a dark place and there seems no end to

In a dark place

'The enemy pursues me, he crushes me to the ground; he makes me dwell in darkness like those long dead.'
(Psa. 143:3)

the problems that life is throwing at you, take heart, be truthful and tell God about it. Allow Him to come into your situation, place His loving arms around you and comfort you. Notice that 'in the darkness' (v.3) is exactly where the enemy would have you be. However, the psalmist knew of God's unfailing love for him (v.8), and we need likewise to hold on to that truth. God loves each of us more than words can say. In fact, that was my experience: God heard my cry and turned my situation around. In the same way, Jesus came so that you could be released from the dark places today (Isa. 61:1).

Lord, thank You that You love me unconditionally, whatever circumstances I am in. Amen.

DAY 159

PSALM 144;
ISAIAH 49:15

'Excuse me, your face is familiar, don't I know you from somewhere?' It was the usual opener and our conversation in the Mess was followed by a whirlwind discussion of various postings, dates and cap badges until the jackpot was hit. 'Oh, *you* lived next door to so and so!' Hours afterwards, my memory burned as I relived precious times in faraway places, recalling old friends and forgotten stories. Memories can be so fickle (or perhaps it's just my own!). I move house and move on, forgetting so much that was important in the process.

In verse 4, the psalmist describes our days as if they were 'a breath ... like a fleeting shadow'. Sometimes, my memories can feel like that. How wonderful then, that God is not like that. Despite the fact that in the context of eternity, our lives are shorter than a

Don't I know you?

'Lord, what are human beings that you care for them, mere mortals that you think of them?' (Psa. 144:3, NIV, 2011)

heart-beat, He thinks of us. He never forgets us, no matter how long it has been or how far we have wandered. In fact, it is harder for Him to forget about us than it is for a mother to forget her own child (Isa. 49:15). He remembers every last detail about us, right down to the number of hairs on our heads (Luke 12:7). The only thing He has total amnesia about is the sins that we have repented of: they are completely forgiven and forgotten (Heb. 8:12).

Consider: God is there for me even when I forget that Jesus is the best friend I could ever have, and become blasé about His limitless love and constant mercy. He is still there when I drift away and then feel guilty about renewing our friendship. He is here for me today.

DAY 160

PSALM 145;
HEBREWS 13:8

Trusting God's character

'The Lᴏʀᴅ is faithful to all his promises and loving toward all he has made.' (Psa. 145:13)

One of the camps I lived on whilst serving in the RAF before I became a Christian, had the women's accommodation block located near to the station church. I'd sometimes think about going over to the church to speak to the padre and, although I never did, I often used to think about God. I'd had quite a moral upbringing and used to go to church when I was younger. Whilst I was serving in the Military that all changed, however, as living away from my parents gave me a new-found freedom. I no longer had to justify my actions and choices to them but could do as I pleased.

I thought I would be happier, but in truth it changed me into a somewhat sad, uncaring and rather immoral individual. This experience led me to the decision to leave the RAF prematurely and to have an HIV test. I was fearful as I waited for the test results and I cried out to God for a second chance, promising I would live the way *He* wanted if He would bring the results back negative. God graciously answered that desperate prayer and I became a Christian about four years later. God *is* faithful and He *is* loving and, despite the difficulties we might experience in life, His character never changes. Being a Christian can be a challenge so if you find yourself struggling, consider God's character. He is worth trusting, whatever has happened in the past and whatever the current circumstances are. His forgiveness and love are *always* freely available.

Lord, I turn to You today. Thank You for Your love and forgiveness. Amen.

DAY 161

PSALM 146;
2 CORINTHIANS 12:9

This psalm is one of hope that the Lord is in control of every part of our lives and we just need to trust Him. I was given an assignment when I was working at the Army Personnel Centre in Glasgow: I was to be a Project Leader to set the IT Policy. I am no IT guru, indeed I had a fear of IT at the time and frankly I did not even understand the title of the project. I fought the Lord, my boss and everyone else *not* to have this task because I felt I was inadequate and caged in! I was ordered to do it and felt controlled, with no choice in the matter and very vulnerable because I did not have the gifting for the task. Now I realise *that* is the very time when the Lord really wants to demonstrate His power.

One evening as I walked to church the Lord spoke to me: 'My grace is sufficient for you.' It was absolutely clear, and I

God equips and provides

'The LORD sets prisoners free, the LORD gives sight to the blind, the LORD lifts up those who are bowed down, the LORD loves the righteous.' (Psa. 146:7–8)

knew He would equip me and I was free to do this with His help. I worked with an amazing team whom the Lord provided and, with the right expertise alongside me, I finished well; it was completed not in my strength but in the Lord's! I had felt oppressed at the beginning but I was invigorated and free at the end. Why don't you ask God to equip you more fully today for the work He has called you into?

Lord Jesus, when I feel controlled, let down, inadequate and oppressed, please speak to me and reassure me that Your grace is sufficient for me. Help me to be real with You and accept Your rescue plan. Amen.

DAY 162

PSALM 147;
JAMES 1:17

As a child, my father used to take us out into the farmyard and teach us to recognise the Plough in the night sky. He then showed us how to use this to find Polaris, or the North Star, which would help us know which way we were facing, wherever we were in the Northern hemisphere.

As well as being a useful navigational aid, it became a symbol of security for me, and also gave me a sense of closeness, especially when I was away from home at boarding school. As I moved even further away with the Army, I would search for the Plough and be reminded that my family was under the same group of stars and might even be looking at the same patch of stars at the same time.

God also promises to us that He will look after us no matter where in the universe we are – we may feel far from

Our spiritual compass

'He determines the number of the stars and calls them each by name.' (Psa. 147:4)

friends and family and that the world is a big, bad, scary place; but God is bigger than that and can hold each of us in His hands. He also gave us His Word, to show us the way, to point us in the right direction and to keep us on His path, as we ask for His guidance and for our will to be more closely aligned to His.

Lord, thank You that You know us and love us, wherever we are in the world, and wherever we are spiritually. Help me to trust in Your Word, to continually check the direction in which I'm heading and to walk in Your way. Amen.

DAY 163

Amazing creation

'Let them praise the name of the LORD, for he commanded and they were created.'
(Psa. 148:5)

On the drive back to boarding school, my fifteen-year-old daughter was revising for her science GCSE. 'Mum, did you know that polar bears' fur isn't white but transparent?' she asked me. I had to confess that I didn't. I then learnt that the pads of their feet were fur-lined. I realised again in that brief conversation that there is so much still to learn about the wonder and intricacy of this kingdom of God we inhabit; myriads of diverse creatures all perfectly adapted to live in all kinds of terrain and temperatures.

Against this vast background we can marvel, 'What is man that you are mindful of him ...?' (Heb. 2:6). Seeing the deliberate hand of a purposeful Creator behind all aspects of creation invites us 'mere humans' to take up the responsibility of careful stewardship of this earth; an impossible task until we look to Jesus crowned with glory and honour. While at present, we do not see everything on this earth subject to His Lordship, we have the certain hope that one day all creation *will* be fully restored to glory.

In the meantime we are left with the challenge of how we can be better stewards of this earth; whether that is in more careful use of the available recycling facilities, planting a few more trees and flowers in the spartan married quarters we inhabit, or giving more generously to humanitarian aid efforts which seek to bring relief to those areas of the world badly hit by disasters. I know for myself that there is more I can do, what about you?

Creator God, show me how to glorify You in the way I live. Amen.

DAY 164

I had hit rock bottom: I put the crying baby in the cot, shut the door, turned on the hoover, ran downstairs, turned on the radio, television and every other noise-making kitchen appliance, climbed under the desk and sobbed. My husband found me there when he came home from work soon afterwards. Post-natal depression is awful and ever since that time I have struggled not to sink back into depressive behaviour. In that battle one of the most effective weapons has been the weapon of praise.

Praise forces me to look up, to look beyond myself, to look at God who loves me and cares for me and is *so much bigger* than the issues and problems I find myself struggling against. It is not easy to praise from a place of depression and sometimes it is the hardest thing in the world to force the words out. I find that reading some

The power of praise

'May the praise of God be in their mouths and a double-edged sword in their hands ...' (Psa. 149:6)

of the Psalms aloud during these times is one of the best ways to praise God. At other times it helps to put on some praise and worship music. At times like these, choosing to praise is an act of will. It is like picking up a sword and beginning to fight the enemy. The walls of Jericho fell when the people praised God with loud shouts of praise and trumpet blasts. What are the walls surrounding you today? Have you tried picking up the weapon of praise by worshipping God despite the circumstances? Why not try it today?

Lord Jesus, I choose to worship and praise You today, for You are worthy of honour and praise. Amen.

DAY 165

PSALM 150;
1 CORINTHIANS 12

I enjoy listening to music, but I'm not good at playing instruments and I'm even worse at singing. On church parades when surrounded by men who don't want to sing, I really struggle to find the right key! So Psalm 150 did very little for me for years. Recently, I was awoken early by the sun streaming through the window, accompanied by the sounds of sparrows chirping. In the nearby wood, woodpeckers were hammering on a tree. It was a beautiful mix of sounds, rather like a symphony. However, it would be useless if the sparrows tried to hammer, the woodpeckers to shine, or the sun to chirp; each knows its talents and has its own way of praising the Creator. Psalm 150 contains the same truth: it doesn't matter whether we are musical or not, we can still praise God. As 1 Corinthians 12 reminds us, we don't need to try to be like

Praise the Lord!

'Let everything that has breath praise the Lord. Praise the Lord.' (Psa.150:6)

anyone else, not even our colleagues or neighbours, because God has created us uniquely.

As we come to the end of our times of 'coffee with God' our prayer is that you will have encountered God in a new, deeper and more personal way. We have so many reasons to praise Him so, whether your way is through singing, shouting, humming, dancing, playing an instrument or praying, allow yourself to be carried away by the love and wonder of God and to praise Him with all your might!

Lord, thank You for the beauty and diversity of Your creation; help me to grow into the person You created me to be, through Your love and power. I praise You, Almighty God. Amen.

Glossary of military terms

AFCU – Armed Forces' Christian Union – a tri-Service, all-ranks, UK Military Christian fellowship. With its roots in the Army Prayer Union, established in 1851, the AFCU is primarily a prayer union that exists to support its members in prayer and to provide opportunities for fellowship.

BATUS – acronym for British Army Training Unit Suffield – a large training area used by British troops in Canada.

Bergen – type of rucksack issued to UK military.

Blue-job – domestic chore better suited to a man.

Bluey – free air-letter. Now also available as an 'e-bluey' – this special type of email is printed out at its destination and delivered as regular post. Some BFPOs also offer a 'fax-bluey' service.

BFPO – British Forces Post Office.

Chuff chart – calendar showing the number of days left until a specific event, usually the end of an operational tour.

Exercise – military deployment for training purposes.

Fear naught – Royal Tank Regiment motto.

IED – improvised explosive device.

Leads – Officer training involves a large number of problem-solving exercises in the field where one member of the syndicate is nominated as leader, briefed on the situation and then expected to come up with possible solutions. Having been given 'the lead', the trainee officer then has to organise the rest of the syndicate so that the problem is solved within a given time limit.

March-in – term used to describe process of taking over a married quarter.

March-out – term used to describe the inspection of a married quarter when moving out.

Mastiff – British armoured vehicle.

OC – Officer Commanding – army position usually held by a major in charge of a company or squadron.

OCF – Officers' Christian Fellowship (US military fellowship).

Op/Ops – slang for operation.

Op Tour – operational deployment usually lasting six months but can extend to a year.

Patch – group of co-located military houses.

RMP – Royal Military Police.

Soft target – military term referring to an un-armoured person or thing.

'Stand to' – a command to take a position of readiness.

Theatre – term used to describe location of a military operation.

Tour – military job or posting usually lasting 2–3 years.

Wardroom – Naval Mess.

XO – Executive Officer (Naval position).

Meet the authors

Carole Backhouse

Carole served in the WRNS for nine years where she became a Christian. She married a Naval Officer who is now a Padre. They have a teenage son. During her time in the Military she has lived in Italy, Australia and Canada.

Carole enjoys walking and baking cakes for sailors.

Tracey Bateson

Tracey has been in the Army for four years as a Padre. As someone who does not like ironing or camping, no one was more surprised than she, to be called to this ministry!

Tracey doesn't like the smell of her new baby's nappy but she loves his smiles and coos!

Sian Campbell-Colquhoun

Sian is married to Ben, a Royal Engineer, and has three children. She's lived in eight different houses in ten years. Since becoming a Christian aged 17 on a Welsh mountain, she has enjoyed organising events that welcome new families to church.

Sian loves doing children's parties and making bunting.

Berenice Ducker

Berenice trained as a dog handler in the Royal Air Force Police. This prepared her for God's calling to be an evangelist to the British Military following her commitment to Christ.

She has a passion for animals and adores her 17-year-old cat. With Berenice there's no plan B!

Jo Eaton

Jo was an Army Nurse before marrying her military husband 28 years ago. She has spent much of that time living in Germany bringing up their two children. She loves praying with people and encouraging them in their faith.

Jo enjoys bird watching, walking in the mountains and solving puzzles.

Beanie Farrimond

Beanie served in the Army for 16 years and became a Christian after serving with other Christians. Beanie now works as a Children's and Families' Worker for her local church.

Beanie loves her two young children and the challenges posed by renovating their new home (except for the dust!).

Val Hall

Val is married and, for 27 years, served in the Army. She now works for the AFCU and counts it a privilege to see God at work in the Armed Forces.

Val is a keen horsewoman who has ridden for England and been reserve for the British Endurance team.

Julie Hamilton

Julie has only ever known Army life, being first an Army daughter and then the devoted wife of a serviceman for 32 years. Having five grown-up children, she has many a comical tale to share concerning Christian family life.

Julie enjoys long walks and agrees 'Silence is golden'.

Lynn Hayler

Lynn has been the wife of a serving RAF frontline pilot for the last 20 years. She has one teenage daughter away at boarding school.

Lynn is passionate about seeing lives changed by Christ. She has a Springer Spaniel puppy who keeps her feet firmly grounded (and wet and muddy!).

Julie Knox

Julie, a television news reporter with British Forces Broadcasting, has lived in military communities overseas and joined troops on operations. She became a Christian during her youth in Northern Ireland, where her sprightly grandfather taught her water-skiing.

Julie relishes extreme assignments, like parachuting with the Red Devils and road-testing tanks.

Lynnette Macmillan

Lynette trained as a nurse and works at a military medical centre looking after soldiers and their families. She is married to a soldier in the RAMC and has two children.

Lynette likes long meandering walks and reading but is happiest whilst experimenting with creative cooking.

Caroline Maggs

Caroline served in the British Army for four years. She is an Army wife and mother. Caroline became a Christian after a good friend was killed in Bosnia. She enjoys showing God's love to others in practical ways.

Caroline loves searching for seasonal food in the hedgerows and making macaroons.

Leah Middlewick

Leah is currently serving in the RAF. She loves outdoor activities and feels closest to God in this environment.

Don't be fooled by her diminutive size – Leah is a real tomboy at heart and likes to think she can take on any guy in a press-up competition!

Amanda New

Amanda grew up in an Army family and has worked as Office Administrator for the AFCU for the last 23 years. She enjoys the pastoral side of leading a home group and one-to-one time with friends.

Amanda loves photographing nature and doing cross-stitch to commemorate friends' special occasions.

Hayley Palmer

Hayley is the wife of an RAF pilot. They have two children. When she is not busy with her family she enjoys spending time sharing the gospel with children and encouraging families in their faith.

Hayley loves dancing and experimenting in the kitchen, usually with some success ...!

Liesel Parkinson

Liesel has been an Army wife for the last 19 years; most of that time has been in Germany. She leads the Ladies' Ministry for the AFCU along with serving as a Methodist Local Preacher in the Garrison Church.

Liesel likes hot summers, teapots and the smell of fresh laundry.

Carrie Priestnall

Carrie became a Christian 14 years ago after attending an Alpha course. She met Steve in Cologne when he was stationed at RAF Brüggen and has now enjoyed 12 years of being an RAF wife. They have 8-year-old twins.

Carrie loves autumn walks and long summer evenings.

Jan Ransom

Jan left the British Army in 2002 after 26 years of service, and founded a ministry called Flame International. She now travels the world ministering to the broken-hearted in countries traumatised by war, genocide or oppression.

Jan loved her time in the Army and loves what she does now even more!

Julie

Lynnette

Caroline

Leah

Amanda

Hayley

Liesel

Carrie

Jan

Vicky Roberts

Vicky has been an Army Officer for 19 years, in 17 locations including Bosnia and Kosovo. She is married with two children. God's influence in her life has increased throughout her military career, especially through the miracle of her new baby.

Vicky likes wildlife, classic vehicles, tennis and cream teas.

Katja Samuel

Katja served in the Royal Navy for 12 years; this involved being a Logistics Officer in diverse operational theatres and a Legal Adviser. Since leaving the Navy, she has specialised in international human rights and conflict-related matters.

Katja enjoys most types of cake, especially chocolate and lemon-flavoured ones.

Natalie Sawtell

Natalie was born in South Africa, moving to the UK 17 years ago. She is an Army wife and has two children.

Natalie is the 'Charity Shop Queen' and loves baking and holding tea parties for her friends and family using all the crockery she has bought.

Karen Sharma

Karen has been an Army wife for 26 years, involving herself with women's fellowship, Sunday School and home groups in military garrisons worldwide. She has three children and three grandchildren – all of whom are her great delight.

Golfing, hiking and her family keep Grandma Karen young in body and spirit!

Clare Shaw

Clare served in the Royal Navy for four years. Now she is a Naval wife, mother of two and a GP. She became a Christian at university whilst trying to prove God didn't exist.

Despite being scared of heights, Clare will happily hang on wires out of search and rescue helicopters.

Kate Smith

Kate is an Army wife of 17 years and mother of two. She is a counsellor, has a passion for seeing people's lives released through God's healing and a heart for Israel and the Jewish people.

Kate loves hair straighteners, fluffy hot water bottles and drinking a latte with friends.

Katherine Twigg

Katherine has served in the Royal Navy for 15 years. Leaning on her faith for encouragement throughout operational life, she is a listener who has often been nicknamed 'the counsellor' on board ship.

Katherine enjoys the freedom of hill walking, and would love to have her own dog one day!

Catherine Walton

Catherine was married to a soldier for 14 years. Now divorced, she is a single mother of two beautiful teenage girls. Although brought up in a Christian home she came to a personal faith while posted in Germany.

Catherine enjoys patchwork, loves walking and spends many happy hours camping.

Kerry Watt

Kerry has been in the Army for 8 years, serving as a doctor in Birmingham and Yorkshire. She belongs to a local Pentecostal church where her main activities are kids' work/riot control, and audience participation.

Kerry likes jumping from rock to rock by the river, and coloured pens.

Joan Weaver

Joan is the wife of an Army Chaplain and mother of four. She seeks to use the listening ear God has given her to support struggling mums and young children within the Army community.

Joan loves the way patchwork quilting combines beautiful patterns and colours with warmth and usability.

Vicky
Katja
Natalie
Karen
Clare
Kate
Katherine
Catherine
Kerry
Joan

Your chuff chart

1	2	3	4	5	6	7	8	9	10	11	12	13	14
15	16	17	18	19	20	21	22	23	24	25	26	27	28
29	30	31	32	33	34	35	36	37	38	39	40	41	42
43	44	45	46	47	48	49	50	51	52	53	54	55	56
57	58	59	60	61	62	63	64	65	66	67	68	69	70
71	72	73	74	75	76	77	78	79	80	81	82	83	84
85	86	87	88	89	90	91	92	93	94	95	96	97	98
99	100	101	102	103	104	105	106	107	108	109	110	111	112
113	114	115	116	117	118	119	120	121	122	123	124	125	126
127	128	129	130	131	132	133	134	135	136	137	138	139	140
141	142	143	144	145	146	147	148	149	150	151	152	153	154
155	156	157	158	159	160	161	162	163	164	165	166	167	168
169	170	171	172	173	174	175	176	177	178	179	180		

Little luxuries for those on ops

Practical ideas of things to take or things to send by post ...

Remember, all letters and parcels up to 2kg to operational BFPO addresses are FREE – speak to your local Post Office for more information.

Music/iPod with great sermon downloads

Kindle with inspiring Christian books

Jelly sweets (that don't melt in the heat!)

Lovehearts – choose your favourite message!

Magazines

Little things for comfort: eg slipper socks

Mini packs of wet wipes/antibacterial hand gel

Cakes and biscuits (homemade fruitcakes and gingernuts will still be fresh when they get there)

Savoury snacks: eg variety nuts, crackers etc

Cooling foot gel – great after wearing boots all day in the heat!

Hot water bottle (it gets cold at night, even in the desert!)

For him: Shower gel and shaving cream
For her: Really nice scent, face cream, soap

Home alone

Ideas for helping/entertaining children during times of separation ...

'Pick a country' – find it on the map, colour in the flag, learn a few words in the language, cook some recipes from the region.

Visit the local library & HIVE information office to find out what is going on in your local area.

Ask your local church about Mother & Toddler and/or Youth groups.

Make a scrapbook of things you and your children get up to or make a memory box to send to your loved one.

Set up a blog page. Mum/Dad on ops can leave special messages for each child. Each child can leave messages for Mum/Dad on ops. A special message for each child keeps each individual relationship with the parent, rather than a general message for all.

Jelly baby 'chuff chart' jars – put in a few extra in case of RAF movement delays!

Check out these two fantastic websites for activities, information and ideas to help you deal with a deployment:

www.combatkidz.co.uk is a great website for children of Service personnel

www.caring-for-combat-kidz.weebly.com is the sister site for parents

Ways to keep in touch

Innovative ways of maintaining strong links with your loved ones during times of separation ...

Before

Record favourite bedtime stories for the children.

Leave a message on your loved one's answer phone.

Make up two small photo albums of your family – one to take on ops; one to leave behind,

Put notes in his/her suitcase to find when they unpack.

During

Old fashioned letter writing (still a hit!). There are also e-blueys you can write on line by logging on to **www.ebluey.com/BFPO**

E-prayers (both ways).

Play chess, making one move a day using e-blueys.

Play Scrabble: player at home keeps the bag of letters. Draw a 'board' on paper. Player on ops has first go. Post the 'board' to each other each time you have a move. Or play Scrabble on Facebook – games can last for days, and it is free!

Plan a holiday together, sharing ideas for a location, accommodation, sports, places you'd like to see together.

Put photos on a memory card and post them out to him/her to view on their camera/computer. Then he/she can return with photos they take whilst on ops.

Send a photo bluey to young children (a picture of Dad or Mum) – better than a letter if they can't read.

Skype, with a webcam.

Book recommendations

If you want to read more, here is an eclectic collection of Christian books that have encouraged and inspired the authors of *Coffee with God*:

Autobiography/Biography

Child of the Covenant –
Michelle Guinness

Faith like Potatoes –
Angus Buchannan

The Happiest People on Earth –
Demos Shakarian

Christian Fiction

A Lineage of Grace – Francine Rivers

Hinds' Feet on High Places –
Hannah Hurnard

Redeeming Love – Francine Rivers

The Screwtape Letters – C S Lewis

Christian Living

Battlefield of the Mind – Joyce Meyer

Captivating – unveiling the mystery of a woman's soul – John & Stasi Eldridge

Enjoying Where You Are on the Way to Where You Are Going –
Joyce Meyer

He Loves Me! Learning to Live in the Father's Affection – Wayne Jacobsen

If You Want to Walk on Water You've Got to Get Out of the Boat –
John Ortberg

Marriage and Parenting

Bringing up Boys – Dr James Dobson

Bringing up Girls – Dr James Dobson

Feminine Appeal: Seven Virtues of a Godly Wife and Mother –
Carolyn Mahaney

Getting Your Kids Through Church: Without Them Ending Up Hating God – Rob Parsons

Making Children Mind Without Losing Yours – Kevin Leman

Making Sense of the Men in Your Life – Kevin Leman

Teenagers – Rob Parsons

The Five Love Languages –
Gary Chapman (editions for children/teenagers also available)

The Sixty Minute Mother –
Rob Parsons

Prayer

A Woman's Guide to Fasting –
Lisa E Nelson

The Power of a Praying Parent –
Stormie Omartian

The Power of a Praying Wife –
Stormie Omartian

The Power of a Praying Woman –
Stormie Omartian

The Armed Forces' Christian Union (AFCU)

Prayerfully serving those who serve

The AFCU is one of a number of British Military Christian organisations. It is an all-ranks, tri-Service organisation of Christians who wish to grow in their faith and share it with those around them.

Prayer: Undergirding everything we do is prayer. A key part of this is that serving members are offered the dedicated consistent prayer support of a group of associate members who pray for them in strict confidence. There are also Bible study or prayer groups running in or near military bases around the world. As a member you will receive information on where and when to find these groups.

In Touch: We seek to put members in touch with one another worldwide, especially on posting. Our address list is produced annually.

Literature: We produce a magazine, 'Contact', teaching material, Bible-reading notes and newsletters for members. Mailings are sent out every two months.

Events: We offer skiing, sailing, family and teenagers' holidays, teaching and equipping weekends, ladies' events and day conferences and marriage courses.

Anyone can join! The only condition for membership is belief in prayer to God through our Lord Jesus Christ and a willingness to pray for the spiritual welfare of the Armed Forces. Whether you are a student heading for the Services, a serving member of HM Forces, a retired serviceman or woman or none of these, you are very welcome!

How to join the AFCU:
Either – Write to or email the AFCU office:
The Armed Forces' Christian Union, Havelock House, Barrack Road, Aldershot, Hampshire, GU11 3NP

Tel: **01252 311221**
Fax: 01252 350722
Email: **office@afcu.org.uk**
Or – Visit our website and join online at: **www.afcu.org.uk**

Inspiring Women Every Day

by various female authors

Daily Bible-reading notes written by women, for women,
to inspire and encourage all ages:

- Increase your faith and ignite your passion for Jesus
- Find practical support to face life's challenges
- Be enlightened by insights into God's Word.

64-page booklet, 120x170mm, published bimonthly
£15.50 UK annual subscription (six issues)
Individual copies: **£2.85 each**

Also available as email subscription/ebook/kindle

Prices correct at time of printing.